A Theology of Conflict and Other Writings on Nonviolence

Dominique Barbé
1931–1988

DOMINIQUE BARBÉ

A Theology of Conflict and Other Writings on Nonviolence

ORBIS BOOKS

Maryknoll, New York 10545

The Catholic Foreign Mission Society of America (Maryknoll) recruits and trains people for overseas missionary service. Through Orbis Books, Maryknoll aims to foster the international dialogue that is essential to mission. The books published, however, reflect the opinions of their authors and are not meant to represent the official position of the society.

Part I of this book was originally published as *Uma Teologia do Conflito: A Não-Violência ativa* © 1985 by Edições Loyola, Rua 1822 n. 347, Caixa Postal 42.335, 04216 – São Paulo – SP, Brazil
The essays "Grace and Power" and "Why Active Nonviolence in Brazil?" were originally published in *La grace et le pouvoir*, © 1982 by Éditions du Cerf, 29 bd Latour-Maubourg, Paris and in *A graça e o poder*, © 1983 by Edições Paulinas, São Paulo. They appeared in English in *Grace and Power*, © 1987 by Orbis Books, Maryknoll, NY 10545
The essay "Christ and Politics" was originally published in *A Firmeza-Permanente*, © 1977 by Edições Loyola, São Paulo
English translation © 1989 by Orbis Books, Maryknoll, NY 10545
All rights reserved
Manufactured in the United States of America

Manuscript editor: William E. Jerman

Library of Congress Cataloging-in-Publication Data

Barbé, Dominique.
    A theology of conflict and other writings on nonviolence /
Dominique Barbé: translated from the Portuguese by Robert R. Barr
and others.
    Bibliography: p.   cm.
    ISBN 0-88344-546-8
    1. Nonviolence – Biblical teaching.   2. Violence – Psychological
aspects.   3. Liberation theology.   I. Title.
BS680.N6B36   1989
241'.697 – dc20   89-8827
                                                                    CIP

Contents

PART TWO
NONVIOLENCE AND THE GOSPEL

Chapter 12
**TRANSFORMING LOVE: AN INTERVIEW WITH
DOMINIQUE BARBÉ**

NOTES

Foreword

What can a North American learn from Dominique Barbé, liberation theologian of the Christian base communities of Brazil, from this, his final work?

Knowing of Barbé's recent death, I read *The Theology of Conflict* as his last telegram from the heart of the world. Barbé was a priest living in the immense suffering and confusion of a slum on the outskirts of São Paulo, Brazil. He wrote his books on the theology of nonviolent liberation with the midnight discipline of one whose 24-hour ministry was with the suffering poor of the base communities he helped form. Out of that ministry have come two concise works published in this country, *Grace and Power* and now *The Theology of Conflict*. The interview included in the present work has a particular intensity suggesting the author's sense that this might well be his last word, although he seems also to have lived every day in that awareness. What we are given by Dominique Barbé in his final telegram from the heart of the world is a message of nonviolent transformation.

Liberation of the suffering is the Latin American message with which Barbé thoroughly identified, seeing liberation theology as a great practical and theoretical step beyond Marxism — a revolutionary religious theory. Yet as proud as he was to be identified as a proponent of liberation theology, Barbé was also consciously pushing that theological revolution into something new. Perhaps living in a *favela* (shantytown) helped give Barbé the extra motivation to force his own consciousness to the edge of a revolutionary theology, then over that edge into a new possibility seen in this book, which can now only be developed by others.

Barbé's new idea surfaces periodically in *The Theology of Conflict,* like a creature from the depths of the sea wanting to fly.

The idea is not only nonviolence, an idea that in Barbé achieves the Gandhian plane of militant mysticism, especially in the words of his interview. From the urgency of his base communities, Barbé's nonviolence emerges as a Latin American synthesis of resistance and contemplation, a Brazilian counterpart to what was born in Gandhi through his parallel experiment in living out the suffering of India.

To see biblically in a Brazilian slum what Gandhi saw through the lens of his ashram is itself a significant step for liberation theology and for us all. Yet Barbé's new idea is more than a liberation nonviolence with its own fusion of militance and mysticism. The "something more," the creature from the depths wanting to fly, was known by Gandhi, too. In *Grace and Power* and *The Theology of Conflict,* Barbé is probing its reality in the gospel, where Gandhi went further than almost any Christian, yet was blocked by doctrines so distorted by missionaries that he never reached the Christian equivalent of satyagraha. Barbé is there, kneeling beside Jesus, straining to see what his master is writing on the ground. Has Barbé seen that new word? Can we see it, too?

The word seems to be transformation.

It comes to us as a question, a question sharpened by the suffering in a *favela.*

Can God do more than liberate the suffering from their enemies? Can God transform persons in a way that will transform their enemies? Is there in the nuclear age a new creation about to occur, a good news of nonviolent transformation known already by Jesus and Gandhi, suggested by Barbé in his unfinished work?

Barbé says Christians cannot know that new creation without knowing, for the first time perhaps, the truth of the resurrection.

We are at the end of our theology. Barbé is saying more than you and I want to hear. He is talking about death and life in a way whose North American expression is Vietnam veteran Brian Willson being run over by a U.S. Navy weapons train, then returning to the tracks, without his legs, to say he has compassion for the train crew.

"Love your enemies (who blow up Nicaraguan children), do good to those who hate you (and cut off your legs). . . ."

Brian Willson, another pilgrim of the absolute, has like Dominique Barbé broken through to the reality of transformation. The way Willson puts it in our North American context is in terms of the same systemic enemy as determines the fate of those in the *favela:*

> I'm in a position now where I feel incredibly liberated because I've been put on the terrorist list. They've monitored all my mail and phone calls for the past 14 months, they've taken off my legs, they've fractured my skull, and they've threatened to put me in jail for tax resistance. They can do whatever they're going to do, and I'm going to keep doing what I'm doing because I believe in it. And if I'm in jail or dead or have my arms taken off, I feel like I've found a place in the universe that's whole and feels clean.

Dominique Barbé's gospel word of transformation is the good news of the cross and resurrection, the news on the tracks that we will be run down if we plant ourselves firmly enough in front of the train, as Brian Willson did. This is good news because transformation, resurrection, comes with the train. They will run us down. But "they" are we. We in North America are the train. Our train is running over Barbé's *favela* and the entire world. We need to plant our lives directly in front of that train of ours in order to stop it—to be transformed, as the world will be transformed. Losing our lives to the train (in a variety of ways) is transformation, resurrection, God's creation of the new humanity of the gospel: "For us today resurrection means that life is stronger than death, that good is greater than evil, that grace is stronger than dis-grace."

Barbé draws a comprehensive picture of this resurrection: grace and power, spirituality and politics, inspiration and organization. The way of transformation is all-inclusive and with a binding energy: "The greatest force of revolution is mystical love."

I know two good ways in North America to live out the theology of nonviolent transformation Dominique Barbé suggested in these sporadic writings and had no time to develop further before his death.

The first way is to live as Catholic Worker communities do in the midst of our own slums, where human desperation deepens at the bottom of our warfare state. Our first way of transformation is to respond to the diabolical poverty of capitalism with a transforming evangelical poverty.

The second way of transformation in North America is to confront the warfare state directly with nonviolent civil disobedience, thus joining the poor where so many of them live when they are not on the streets—in prison.

Spanning these two ways of grace is the gospel imperative of organizing loving, nonviolent resistance in every way we can in this society to the systemic murder of humanity being carried out as the foundation of our American way of life: murderous economics in the Third World, murderous economics in U.S. slums, whose root causes are the same as in the Third World.

God alone knows how deeply the evil and suffering for which we are responsible reaches to the heart of the world. But "God alone" is a misnomer. As Barbé has written, the trinitarian God is not alone but lives in and through the love of a community, the human community. That communal Spirit of transformation is rising in humanity. Those who live and die as Dominique Barbé did, at the heart of the world, live now and forever at the heart of God.

Barbé's final telegram from the heart of the world is a message of transformation from the heart of our nonviolent God. We need to act on it.

JAMES W. DOUGLASS

Presentation

Our times are scarcely in need of books. But they are mightily thirsty for witness. With what sounds, noises, and images our ears and eyes are bombarded! What an eagerness to communicate! And yet, for the most part, we are isolated persons. A deathly silence pervades the depths of the human heart, rendering still more impregnable the barriers that divide peoples. Against this stifling, smothering situation of noncommunication, the human person, created in the image and likeness of the Trinity, and therefore made for communion, rises up in protest.

The present volume is scarcely "just another book." It is a life testimony committed to writing. As such, it meets an urgent need on the part of our base church communities and their militant Christians. But it also meets a need experienced by all men and women of good will who struggle to build a more just communion of sisters and brothers. The majority of our people live under oppression. Hunger is not theoretical. Unemployment rots the family from within. A wealthy minority grows ever more wealthy, while the multitudes of the poor become ever more destitute and miserable. We are surrounded by a blind, terribly violent class struggle. Human beings are feeding on the blood of their brothers and sisters.

Cain has institutionalized himself. He has become a system, and now he drinks the blood of Abel, God's suffering people.

Father Dominique Barbé, my friend and brother, was a missionary living in a slum on the outskirts of a city of São Miguel, in the archdiocese of São Paulo. There, in the eye of a hurricane of misery, he experienced in his own flesh the anguish of our people. He was accustomed to conflict. He was not naive on the matter of the class struggle. In the power of the gospel of the Christ whose servant he was, he strove to live the liberating

practice of Jesus. And Jesus never fled conflict. Just the opposite! He met it head on! He became incarnate in a conflict-
ridden society. But he commanded his followers to love their
enemies. And he introduced into the ocean of violence in which
he was immersed the pure water of "active nonviolence"—a
spirit and a method with the potential to create new relationships among God's human creatures: relationships of truth and
justice, and a communion of sisters and brothers.

The living testimony handed on to us by this wonderful book
will give us the strength to resist any kind of servility, and all
compromise between the message of Jesus and the spirit of this
world, which is the spirit of lying, exploitation, and injustice. It
will usher us into the very heart of the salvific deed of Jesus
Christ, who surrendered himself utterly to a God who is "our
Father" as well as his—a Father who makes us all sisters and
brothers of one another in making us his daughters and sons,
and who requires of us that we act in a manner consistent with
our faith by providing all of our brothers and sisters with their
daily bread. Nothing that fails to build a humanity of solidarity
and communion has a place in the work and life of Christ, the
Redeemer of the human race. Hence the insistence with which
Father Barbé repeats one of the most revolutionary lines in the
gospel: "The Sabbath was made for humankind, not humankind
for the Sabbath" (Mark 2:27)! In other words, when law ceases
to serve human beings, law should be disobeyed.

As a disciple of Christ crucified, Father Barbé proclaimed the
resurrection. This testimony, lived at the heart of the struggle
of the people, and now consigned to writing, will be provocative!
Not all will agree with it. As Christians, we must always turn to
the One who proclaimed love and was crucified. Nothing could
be more dangerous for Christians faced with a world in conflict
than the attitude denounced by John in the Book of Revelation:

I know your deeds; I know you are neither hot nor cold.
How I wish you were one or the other—hot or cold! But
because you are lukewarm, neither hot nor cold, I will spew
you out of my mouth! [Rev. 3:15–16].

The ultimate source of *A Theology of Conflict* is the divine
heart of a Father in heaven, bleeding for the suffering in the

lives of his children—children enslaved by the selfishness of their own brothers and sisters, his other sons and daughters! In this situation of conflict, the book in your hands will be a sure guide along the path of liberation. For that path is one of active nonviolence!

I give thanks to God for this vibrant testimony, now consigned to writing and thereby placed at the service of the building of a more just communion of sisters and brothers.

BISHOP ANGÉLICO SÂNDALO BERNARDINO
SÃO PAULO

A Theology of Conflict
and Other Writings
on Nonviolence

Introduction

Christian metaphysics is essentially trinitarian. It is based on an extremely original conception of God, one found nowhere else in the history of human thought. It is based on the notion that God is Love (1 John 4:8, 16). In other words, it proclaims a God who is Difference—but without any separation between the differing elements, as also without their confusion. I can love someone only if that someone is different or distinct from myself, and yet face to face with me—neither absorbed by me, surely, nor, on the other hand, separated or withdrawn from me. This is also what the Council of Chalcedon (A.D. 451) says of the divine and human natures of Christ! "We profess one and the same Christ Jesus, the only-begotten Son, having two natures, without confusion or transformation or separation between them." The two natures of Christ, or his two wills, like the three Persons of the Holy Trinity, are neither confused nor separated.

The societal consequences are incalculable. It is the tragedy of our society that it either absorbs or isolates its members, either exploits or marginalizes them. Our society is the very opposite of the Holy Trinity. Ours is an *atrinitarian* society. A society animated by the divine grace would surely neither separate the human persons who compose it (by isolating and marginalizing them) nor confuse them (by absorption and exploitation).

"God is Love" means that within God exists the will to abide in the "other" without either confusion or division. Walter Kasper explains: if God is free in love, then God's love is not spent, exhausted, among Father, Son, and Spirit. Rather, there is still

Translated by Robert R. Barr.

room for the world and the human being. The fundamental Christian metaphysical intuition is its replacement of a metaphysics of *being* with a metaphysics of *subject-in-relation*, a subject in expansion in history. The basis of reality is a subject-in-relation. The axis of history, then, turns on communion.

A practical consequence of this is that there can never be a merely political solution to the political problem. We hear the call for a new republic, and total democracy. Yes, surely; but let us be clear about the *theology* of the political problem. We must realize that what we are doing is seeking to actualize a "trinitarian" society—one in which persons are neither exploited (confounded with one another and simply "used up") nor marginalized (separated from the "haves"). Such a society will be the fruit not simply of a political or administrative effort, but of grace, and of an openness to the divine grace on the part of all of the members of society. My book, *Grace and Power* (Orbis, 1987), which treats essentially of the theology of liberation and the base church communities, is an attempt to show this mysterious dialectical interplay between human effort and divine inspiration in the area of the political and the social.

Similarly, we shall fail to do justice to the question of social *conflict* if we attempt to do so from a point of departure in mere juridical or political considerations. In other words, it is not enough to define the juridical rules of social conflict, that that conflict may transpire in rational fashion. Nor will it suffice to have as one's only goal the strengthening of the power relationships prevailing among the dominated social class, with its various groups, so that this class and these groups may vanquish the oppressor. To be sure, the gospel is no stranger to struggle and conflict. For want of a perception of this, many in the church persist in identifying the commandment of love, which is one thing, with class collaboration, which is another matter. In order to be faithful to the gospel, and to the manifestation of the divine design that seeks a society of full participation, we shall have to renounce this identification, and restore "charity" to its correct historical place—that is, its place in social conflict—if we are ever to mold a society that will transcend the domination of one class by another. Liberation theology has reflected too little on the theology of conflict. In this book, I hope to carry this reflection forward.

PART ONE

A Theology of Conflict

Chapter 1

The Logic of the Scapegoat

You have heard the commandment, "An eye for an eye, a tooth for a tooth." But what I say to you is: offer no resistance to injury. When a person strikes you on the right cheek, turn and offer him the other. If anyone wants to go to law over your shirt, hand him your coat as well. Should anyone press you into service for one mile, go with him two miles. Give to the man who begs from you. Do not turn your back on the borrower.

Love your enemies.

—Matthew 5:38–42, 44

It is my conviction that the Bible gradually presents a new practice of conflict. To be sure, the evolution is a slow one. We all know that the appearance of the "new" in the evolution of living species—and cultures—is rarely easy to perceive. A particular trait begins to change, slowly and gradually. After a long period of time, it acquires a critical consistency—and finally the animal or plant makes a "quantum leap." We may use the analogy of a railroad switch. Two trains come to a switch—their "parting of the ways." At first there is no great difference be-

---

Translated by Robert R. Barr.

5

tween their new routes. Indeed any divergence may be all but imperceptible. But as time goes on, and the tracks spread farther and farther apart, the trains may eventually head in opposite directions.

Thus it is that, slowly at first, then with a bound, a crucial change occurs in the approach prescribed by the Bible for the resolution of conflict. A new "practice" appears. We must re-read the Bible from the point of view of Jesus, or of Isaiah 53, and not merely from that of Moses, which would be a backward, genuinely "reactionary" reading to be making in these New Covenant times of ours.

The thesis I seek to defend is simple: no compulsory human sacrifice, be it that of the most horrid of monsters, can eliminate violence from human societies. Only the *freely offered* sacrifice of the righteous one can eliminate that violence. We must move from the logic of the scapegoat — that of the compulsory sacrifice — to the logic of the Lamb of God — that of the freely offered sacrifice of the innocent one, the righteous one.

This is what we have in Jesus' familiar words about a love of enemies — the gospel passage immediately following the words of the epigraph to this chapter:

> You have heard the commandment, "You shall love your countryman but hate your enemy." My command to you is: love your enemies, pray for your persecutors. This will prove that you are sons of your heavenly Father, for his sun rises on the bad and the good, he rains on the just and the unjust. If you love those who love you, what merit is there in that? Do not tax collectors do as much? And if you greet your brothers only, what is so praiseworthy about that? Do not pagans do as much? In a word, you must be made perfect as your heavenly Father is perfect.

But we must be careful not to read this passage apart from its historical context. We must not seek to understand it in disjunction from the slow historical evolution that explains its appearance. The text should not be torn from the tissue of history.

In order the better to be able to make a nonviolent rereading of the Bible from the point of view of Jesus and the more "evangelical" prophets, let us first consider the remarkably original anthropological hypothesis of René Girard, which, it seems to me, provides extremely interesting interpretive keys for many facets of human life.[1]

My own study will not attempt to analyze conflict from a starting point in the class struggle. Nor will it be my intent to confront hominization in terms of a dialectical struggle with nature. Rather we shall read history in terms of some of its *symbols*. We shall see what type of symbols, on the level of ideology, have been used in human history for the resolution of human conflict. Of course, one reading does not exclude another. Perhaps, then, our philosophical presupposition will be the "ideological instance" — the human capacity for creating ideas and symbols. After all, this ideological instance is fully as determinative for an orientation of history as the economic or political instances would be.

ANTHROPOLOGICAL HYPOTHESIS OF RENÉ GIRARD

The Human Mimetic Faculty

One of our most remarkable human qualities, Girard begins, is our *imitative faculty*. Among all the animals, *Homo sapiens* is the one with the most prodigious gift for observation, as well as for reproducing the act observed. Girard opens his work with Aristotle's maxim: "The human being differs from the other animals by reason of a greater capacity for imitation" (*Poetics*, 4). Through an analysis of the human mimetic faculty, we shall see that this faculty generates, at one and the same time, both *culture* (learning) and *violence*. Anyone can perform the experiment. Put several children in the same room with a large number of toys. Strange and illogical as it may seem, no matter how many toys lie about, the children will simply have to have the toys in one another's hands! And there will be a tussle.

Girard explains. This is not the sign of a particularly bellicose nature. It is only the manifestation of one animal species' exceptional capacity for imitation. What one member of the group does, the other wishes to do as well. And this in turn explains the prodigious growth of human culture. By observing, registering, and imitating the behavior of their fellows, human beings, more than any other animal, amass an enormous quantity of information, and a huge number of solutions for the difficult problems of human survival.

The learning of human language, for example, is nothing more than the imitation by the child of the vocal signs emitted by its parents (who have themselves inherited them) in order to be able to respond to the mighty needs, functions, and perils of existence. The other animals proceed in this same fashion. There is an animal "language," learned in the animal's immature years. But in the human species, the material to be learned is incomparably more extensive, so that the length of time spent in the imitation of one's elders in the art of communication becomes enormous — the time required to receive the entire legacy of past discoveries.

We shall also see, later, why human culture, more than any other animal "togetherness," attains a high level of *complexity* and *consciousness* (compare Teilhard de Chardin's law of complexity-consciousness). The human brain is a huge imitation machine — a computer of incredible sophistication, capable of a rapid assimilation of the complexity of signs and behaviors, together with the accompanying consciousness, whose mental edifice composes human culture.

Once more we observe the *ambivalent* nature of learning, so frequently confirmed by experience. I can learn rapidly only by imitation — by observing, in a *model person*, a behavior or teaching that I look upon as an intelligent manner of conducting myself or of knowing reality. The object of the knowledge of good and evil is always designated by a third party. The model, however, almost always becomes a rival, for in imitating my model I tend to appropriate, seek to gain possession of, what that model does or has. Indeed, I alter, misappropriate, or disfigure, to my taste, what belongs not to me, but to my rival. Thus a little boy loves and admires his father, but opposes him, as well, and enters into competition with him. And the father comes to oppose his rival son. Sooner or later there will be a crisis, and the antagonists will have to delimit their respective space. At least this is what occurs if the crisis is a positive one — for there are negative crises in which the son does not manage to emerge as an original person, or, on the contrary, destroys the work of his father.

A teacher and a disciple are nearly always bound together by a relationship of this nature. The well-known love-rivalry relationship between Freud and Jung is a celebrated case in point. Again we see that imitation, far from being a source of conformism, is, on the contrary, a cause of violence. Aristotle was very perceptive. He saw the latent peril of human *mimesis* — any attempt at imitation of another.

Imitation of Appropriation and of Antagonism

Girard distinguishes two kinds of imitation. One is only moderately violent, the other extremely so. Girard explains that, in any human group, conflicts arise at first through the desire to possess the same object. We have seen that this imitation of appropriation is the necessary condition of learning. But ethnological research likewise reveals that, in the heat of battle, the antagonists come to forget the coveted *object*. Rivalry over an object becomes direct rivalry between persons. Girard calls this second kind of violence, which is far more serious than the first kind, "antagonistic" imitation, for there is no longer any *objective* reason for the conflict: the object has been forgotten.

Now the warring parties are in conflict because the imitation within each impels that person to imitate the violence of his or her neighbor. Precisely what is the basis of their competition now? To my view, the basis of this new spirit of conflict is the desire to gain possession of the "potency," the vital force, that resides within the other. Girard writes:

> We must pursue the logic of the imitative conflict to the very end. The more radical the rivalries become, the more the rivals tend to forget the objects that have caused the conflict to flare up in the first place. Now what fascinates them are each other. Gradually their rivalry has been purified of all that has been external to it — including the object that provoked the competition in the first place. Now their rivalry is basically one of pure prestige. Each rival ends by being the model-obstacle, at once adored and

hated, of the other—the one whom I must level, must consume, at all costs. Mimetism—the human capacity for imitation and learning—has now reached the peak of its strength. But from now on it is exercised no longer on the level of the forgotten object, but as an imitation of the violence of my partner, as pure antagonism, as pure desire to gain possession of this wonderful strength I so fear and admire.[2]

We may have here the deeper explanation of the shocking human customs that concretize the desire to destroy and absorb one's enemy when the mimetic crisis comes to a head. Would this not be the reason for the consumption of human flesh in tribal wars? Ethnology has been telling us for some time that "cannibalism" is a great deal more than the simple consumption of human flesh. The warrior devouring the enemy's flesh does so not in a spirit of bestiality, but in order to absorb that enemy's valor and courage.

Another observation. Is Girard not perhaps emptying conflict of its object—as if the human being never fought for a cause, an objective? And indeed he writes: "Nothing is more difficult to accept than the nothingness and vanity of human conflict, which de facto ends in objectless strife." And he adds, observing the nature of the nuclear threat and the conflicts between the superpowers: "All modern ideologies are simply immense machines calculated to justify and legitimate conflict—which in our day and age can easily annihilate the human race."[3]

In other words, conflict no longer maintains reasonable objectives (objects), for it may so easily annihilate what it claims to defend. Then must all conflict be utterly unreasonable, utterly objectless?

But Girard has never said that all human conflicts are necessarily without a real object. He simply states that human conflict has a strong tendency to forget its object, to become a simple competition among persons. At first I fight for a cause—a just wage, the creation of a party or other organization, the defense of human rights, a more egalitarian society, or the like. But I encounter resistance; and in proportion to the degree of that resistance, my pugnaciousness turns against the person of my enemy. An exclusive will is born within me to do away with this force that resists me, to absorb it and dominate it, even if I must thereby forget or seriously damage the object that has until now constituted the motive of the struggle. This truth is a pregnant one for the *active nonviolent* struggle, one of whose laws must therefore be: in order to calm a violent struggle, I must continually assist the protagonists to turn their attention away from the fascination exercised by the person of the adversary and direct it to the object of contention itself. In sum, I must always ask: *what*, not who, is at stake.

Imitative Crisis and Emergence of the Scapegoat

Once the mimetic struggle comes to a head, a scapegoat must emerge. We may call this phase of the struggle the "stampede." The more acute a struggle becomes, the more members of the antagonistic groups tend to enter the fray. Mimetism, by definition, is contagious: one hand, two hands, three, and so on, reach out to grasp the same object. More and more persons enter the same field of activity. Then the mimetism of appropriation sets the persons themselves at odds with one another. Each begins to forget the object, seeking instead to possess the vital force of the other. Two strike an alliance. Others imitate. Ineluctably, the antagonism escalates.

Concrete experience bears this out. As the mimetic attraction spreads, as it is reinforced with an increasing number of persons maddened by the combat, the moment arrives when one person more than any other appears as being responsible for the violence agitating the community. Then, as the process peaks, the mimetism of antagonism provokes a de facto alliance against a single common enemy. Suddenly the hitherto divided community finds itself *united* against a single individual. The mimetism of appropriation had impelled the members of the group to desire to possess the same object. Now the mimetism of antagonism leads the members of the group to seek the annihilation — and absorption — of their single adversary. Although the mimetism of appropriation *divides*, leading a number of individuals to converge on one and the same object, of which all wish to gain possession, the mimetism of antagonism *unites*, leading these same individuals to converge on the same adversary, whom all now wish to destroy.[4]

Thus the phenomenon of the *scapegoat* appears. The scapegoat, essentially, is a person regarded as guilty, beyond the least doubt, by the community as a whole. The death—or better, the sacrifice—of this person brings peace to the group once more. The group believes that this is how it has expelled the deadly violence that had been destroying it. Therefore there need no longer be any concern with any possible responsibility on the part of the other members of the group, who by definition are innocent now that one only guilty person has been executed. And indeed after the sacrifice of the scapegoat, peace reigns for a time. We shall see, however, that the violence has not been uprooted. The community is deceiving itself.

Let me make three observations here.

First, we cannot know in every case for what reasons, frequently insignificant, this or that victim has been selected to expiate the violence that has been maintaining the community in turmoil. Generally it is someone "different," someone "strange." The scapegoat may be a foreigner, an emotionally disturbed person, a genius, a saint, a prophet, a cripple, a black, a pauper, a prostitute, or the like—anyone marginal, anyone already detached from the body social in some way. There is an illusory, and, at bottom, perverse, intent to purge the community of violence by throwing the blame for the violence on a victim who somehow stands out from the crowd by reason of some special behavior or pitiable status. The actual guilt of the victim is not the main thing at stake.

And this in turn directs our attention to a basic datum of group psychology, one without which the emergence of the scapegoat is radically impossible. In order to qualify for the status and function of scapegoat, the victim selected for the sacrifice must be regarded as guilty beyond the shadow of a doubt, by all members of the group caught up in the crisis. If a single component of the community entertains a suspicion of the innocence, partial or total, of the victim, the struggle may flare up once more.

The gravity of the situation lies in the fact that the unperceived *innocence*, total or relative, of the person accused supposes, as its correlative, that the total or partial guilt of other components of the group has not been discovered. There has been deceit and greed; the threat of a social crisis continues, and the struggle and violence must continue until the true culprits are found out. Then and only then can the roots of the evil at hand be eliminated for good and all. Then and only then will the mechanism of the scapegoat cease to function, inasmuch as some little doubt has been cast on the culpability of the sacrificial victim. Girard puts it admirably: "Genuine scapegoats are those whose guilt is the object of a wall-to-wall belief."[5]

The important thing is not whether the victim is *actually* altogether guilty or not. The important thing is that the victim be *reckoned* to be altogether guilty.

During the French Revolution, King Louis XVI was sentenced to death and beheaded. Once the deed was done, Robespierre, who headed the revolutionaries for the moment, pronounced to the representatives of the nation these typical, and revealing, words: "Louis was king. . . . Now the republic has been founded. And this decides the question before us"—adding, "If Louis is absolved, if Louis is presumed innocent, what becomes of the revolution?"[6] At bottom, then, it mattered very little whether the king was actually a criminal or not. What is important is that the condemnation of one of the antagonists—the king—automatically creates the illusion of the innocence of the other—the revolution.

Louis XVI was executed in classic scapegoat style. A new society was born, and peace—relative peace—returned. Now the protagonists of the drama were persuaded that they had eliminated the one person responsible for the disorder. Actually, as we know, the king was sentenced only by a majority vote, and the lower strata of French society continued to be agitated by a violent class struggle. Thus the way was paved for future disturbances and most profound, enduring social divisions. Meanwhile, an "official" history was established, a consecrated version of the facts, and a certain social order became possible.

In *violent* struggles, accordingly, the victim dies *twice*. Before the scapegoat is put to physical death, it must be slain morally, especially if innocent. Thus the people must believe in the guilt of the one to be condemned. Otherwise, doubt will prevent the return of peace. The sacrificial procedure demands that both the society accepting the murder and the individuals committing it believe in the culpability of those to be executed.[7] Hence the importance of a whole phase of *demoralization*, of calumny, through which the innocent victim must pass.

The case of Jesus is a typical instance. The high priests and the Pharisees, along with Herod's party, want to make Jesus a scapegoat. He must not be an innocent victim, then, a "lamb of God." And so these groups seek to vilify him *politically* ("he is a friend of Caesar") and *religiously* ("this blasphemer wishes to destroy the temple, the holy place of our nation"). Victimization passes by way of incrimination. Hence in a nonviolent struggle it is important to show the innocence of the victim. The community of true disciples are those who, at the price of their lives, testify to the innocence of the persecuted victim, the suffering righteous one.[8]

If the community of disciples manages to see through the diabolical scheme of the mendacious oppressor, who seeks to clothe the innocent with guilt, an important part of public opinion will perceive the victim's innocence. Thus even if the latter must perish, his or her cause will not only survive, but will gain more partisans. Other psychological mechanisms will be set in motion. The masses will be moved at the injustice. The noblest strings of the human heart will be plucked, and their vibrations will generate a new kind of unity and social resistance. A new type of revolution will be launched, as has happened in the case of Poland's Solidarity. But here we are getting ahead of ourselves.

The scapegoat dies not only incriminated, but *compelled*. It does not offer its life freely. Its life is taken. In primitive societies it is a being at once evil and salutary, blessed and cursed: evil because it is regarded as the cause of violence; salutary because its sacrifice brings peace. It is apotheosized after its death, at least in the typical instance. Between violence and the sacred, then, an intimate relationship obtains.

Up to this point we have been engaging in a free commentary on Girard's hypothesis, fleshed out with certain material from our own experience. Girard's most important contribution will be presented in the section that follows. In the meantime, Figure 1 sums up what has been said so far.

Figure 1
How Sacrificial Logic Works

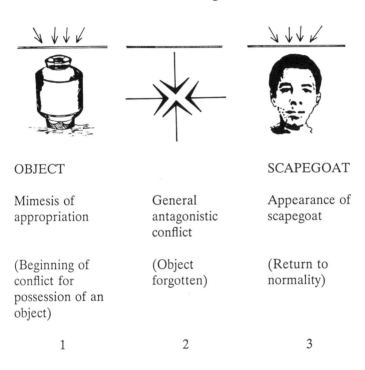

OBJECT		SCAPEGOAT
Mimesis of appropriation	General antagonistic conflict	Appearance of scapegoat
(Beginning of conflict for possession of an object)	(Object forgotten)	(Return to normality)
1	2	3

righteous society vs. incriminated scapegoat

Chapter 2

Prohibitions, Rites, Myths

No society could live, no culture could grow, if the violence born of imitation had continually to be quelled by way of a very costly general crisis involving human sacrifice. Other, more economical, mechanisms are available. We find them in all civilizations, and especially in all religions, says René Girard. The great task of religion, in his opinion, is to keep the peace without having to recur either to the imitative crisis or to the real sacrifice of a scapegoat.

We observe three consistent, convergent methods by which religion channels imitation and prevents it from producing violence. The three basic foundations in all religions are prohibition and taboo, rite, and myth.

PROHIBITION AND TABOO

Places, objects, persons, and times can all be pronounced sacred and be protected by prohibitions. Forbidden objects, spaces, or persons are basically those that otherwise might serve as the object of an imitative rivalry: women, food, weapons, places. All of the members of the same community will be tempted to imitate any member of the group who seeks to gain control of these.

As we have seen, imitation is an ambivalent phenomenon. It

Translated by Robert R. Barr.

consists in learning from one's neighbor, but it is also an invasion of that neighbor. Here the institution of the taboo comes into play. The taboo limits the targets of the community greed, restricts the goals of appropriative imitation. In like manner, certain persons are pronounced sacred. For example, the king, or the women of certain clans, will be protected by a prohibition, to prevent competition for their persons and hence a contagious antagonism among the members of the group. Girard writes:

> The mimesis of appropriation is at the origin of the principal prohibitions—the prohibition of objects, sexual prohibitions, or, once more, dietary prohibitions. The objects of these prohibitions are those objects more accessible to persons living together in community—the women begotten by the group, or the comestibles gathered by the group. These objects are forbidden because, being at every moment physically available to all members of the community, they can momentarily unleash mimetic rivalries capable of placing at risk the survival of the community.[1]

RITE

Second after prohibition, the next foundation of all religion, comes rite. Rite aims at economizing real conflict, and human, flesh-and-blood sacrifice, which are most dangerous procedures for the existence of the group, and which demand a fantastic expenditure of energy. Rite, then, will represent, symbolically, by way of signs of all kinds—dance, cry, song, animal sacrifice—what the community does not wish to relive in reality, because it has already come that route and knows the cost.

What is so surprising, and so dangerous, in rite is its *imitation,* at times in astoundingly realistic ways, of the mimetic crisis that has once torn the community to pieces. For example, a great intratribal battle may be staged as a dance. But will this not be letting the fox into the henhouse? Is such a representation not likely to awaken the ever-present forces of antagonistic, general conflict, and thus issue in real strife? "Would the ritual supper not be an invitation to disaster?"[2] Would rite not produce precisely what the prohibition prevents? Will ritual celebration not incite what prohibition represses?

Here we must return to our analysis of the *sacrificial* resolution of human conflict, in which peace is brought about by the sacrifice of a scapegoat. A ritual celebration, too, must as a general rule culminate in the immolation of a human or animal victim. The elements of the imitative crisis and its resolution must be present in the ritual celebration as well. It is as if the community, having recourse to the celebration, felt some malaise. Prohibitions are inadequate as a means of channeling latent violence. Before there can be a *real* crisis, it is better to have a celebration.

And so the community precisely scouts, lifts, the prohibition — symbolically. It represents, symbolically, that which in normal times is forbidden. But lest the celebration degenerate into actual tragedy, the old solution to the bygone conflict must also be represented: the sacrifice of a victim, a scapegoat. All religions have practiced animal sacrifice — a substitute for human sacrifice. At times, however, the celebration is not satisfied with the animal sacrifice: a human sacrifice is necessary. The Hebrew religion was born in the context of the liturgical sacrifice of Isaac. The Aztecs, along with many other peoples, regularly practiced human sacrifice. Only at this price can celebration escape the greater danger: by a liturgical "staging" of the mimetic crisis that the prohibitions seek to restrain.

MYTH

The third pillar of traditional religion is myth. Put very simply, myth is a "fictional," disguised way of recounting history. The mechanism of reconciliation by way of a scapegoat functions only if the members of the group in which the conflict has occurred believe, without the slightest reticence, in the guilt of the victim immolated. But in reality, in as much as the victim is nearly always (at least partially) innocent, history must be *revised,* in such wise that not the slightest doubt will remain in the collective memory of the tribe or group that has been reestablished after the crisis as to what has placed its existence at risk and what has saved it — the discharging of its sin on the head of an expiatory victim.

Difference between Myth and Reality

Let us now examine, by way of an example, the difference between a mythic and a "real" narrative, the account of an actual fact. Let us compare two texts. The first will recount how the Tikopia people of the Pacific managed, by way of a conflict, to acquire their basic foodstuffs. The second will be a gospel text, likewise relating a conflict — Jesus visiting his family clan in Nazareth, where he preaches in the synagogue, and his relatives try to kill him. In both texts the common point is that *all* unite against *one* to slay the victim (the scapegoat logic). In the gospel text, however, the reality is undisguised, whereas in the Tikopia text it is acceptably "rearranged."

A. Mythical Account of a Lynching among the Tikopia Indians	B. Actual Account of the Lethal Conflict between Jesus and his Family Clan of Nazareth
Once upon a time, when the gods were no different from human beings ... it happened that a foreign god, Tikarau, came to pay a visit to Tikopia, and the gods of that land prepared to welcome him with a most sumptuous banquet. The banquet was preceded by contests of strength and footraces, in which the guest would be invited to demonstrate his prowess. In the midst of one of the races, Tikarau feigned a fall, alleging injury. He rose and began to limp slowly along — then suddenly leapt to the meats that had been	He came to Nazareth where he had been reared, and entering the synagogue on the Sabbath, as he was in the habit of doing, he stood up to do the reading. When the book of the prophet Isaiah was handed him, he unrolled the scroll and found the passage where it was written: "The spirit of the Lord is upon me. ..." Then he began by saying to them, "Today this scripture passage is fulfilled in our hearing." All who were present spoke favorably of him; they marveled at the appealing discourse that came from his lips. They also asked, "Is

heaped upon the table, seized them, and headed for the hills. The family of gods hastened after the thief. This time Tikarau really fell, and the gods of the clan were able to recover the most important dishes that had been prepared for the banquet ... Tikarau managed to vault to the sky with the main dish, but the four vegetable dishes were rescued by the people [Lévi-Strauss, *Totémisme aujourd'hui*].

not this Joseph's son?"

He said to them, "You will doubtless quote me the proverb, 'Physician, heal yourself,' and say, 'Do here in your own country the things we have heard you have done in Capernaum.' But in fact," he went on, "no prophet gains acceptance in his native place. Indeed, let me remind you ... it was to none of [the widows of Isreal] that Elijah was sent, but to a widow of Zarephath near Sidon. ... In the time of Elisha the prophet ... not one [leper in Isreal] was cured except Naaman the Syrian."

At these words the whole audience in the synagogue was filled with indignation. They rose up and expelled him from the town, leading him to the brow of the hill on which it was built and intending to hurl him over the edge. But he went straight through their midst and walked away [Luke 4:16–30].

In the Tikopia myth, the conflict is disguised, but still real. We have the race, the contest of strength, Tikarau's deception, his dexterity in perpetrating it, his thievery, and then the clan's reaction in pursuing him. The expression, "really fell," has an ominous ring. Actually there must have been some horrible scene like a mob lynching in the past. The Tikopia clan must have suffered, in the misty past, a bloody struggle for food, that everlasting object of contention. There must have been some form of competition for food stores (appropriative imitation) until the clan finally reestablished peace through the sacrifice of a scapegoat. As always, the victim, once hated and slain, comes to be sacralized, divinized. He has been the cause of the violence, but also, by his sacrifice, the cause of the group's recovery of peace. Thus the clan exalts him to the skies, raises him to heaven.

It is significant that the victim is so frequently executed by a fall from some great height. Lest they stigmatize themselves by spilling his blood directly—after all, it was family blood—members of the clan would haul the condemned one to the top of a mountain, form a circle around him, and force him to hurl himself into the chasm. Jesus' relatives sought to do the same at Nazareth. The gospel account, however, makes no attempt to disguise the attempted murder. Jesus' relatives are furious that he should recall that, in the past, pagans—and not members of the chosen people—had received divine grace (in the form of the gift of a cure): the widow of Zarephath and Naaman the Syrian. To entertain such a notion is, practically, to commit blasphemy, for it could demolish the whole traditional religious order. The reaction of the clan, then, threatened in its fundamental social and religious equilibrium, is one of extreme irritation. They seek to hurl Jesus over the brow of the hill. True, he passes through their midst and goes his way. But the scene is very nearly that of the murder of a scapegoat. The synagogue has risen up, expelled Jesus from the city, and managed to thrust him to the very brink of the abyss.

In the case of the Tikopia myth, we hear in another account that, as he is dragged to the top of the hill, to the edge of a cliff, Tikarau leaps to heaven with his ill-gotten goods.[3] He can vault to the sky, for he is an *atua*, a god. Had he been a human being, obviously he would have smashed to earth instead! It is not difficult to reconstitute the actual story. Tikarau must have been a tribal member who was cast to his death, as the people of Nazareth sought to do with Jesus. Hence perhaps the sinister concern, in the myth, to emphasize that Tikarau's second fall was altogether real—tragically real.

Thus transformed, the Tikopia story is perfectly acceptable. Tikarau had committed the transgression of stealing food. The ancestors had been right to persecute him, and there is nothing to fear from the victim, who is now a divine being in heaven praying for his executioners! At least this is a reasonable interpretation of the myth in the light of the anthropological hypothesis that we are presenting here.

Growth of Human Culture

It is in this fashion, according to René Girard, that human culture grows and makes progress. Imitation, which generates learning and violence, is channeled by the mechanisms of traditional religion: *prohibition,* which sets limits to imitation by protecting certain persons and objects; *rite,* which reproduces the crisis symbolically (in just the opposite manner from that of prohibition, as it were, so that the celebration requires either a liturgical sacrificial denouement, or else the real sacrifice of a human being or animal substitute); and finally, *myth,* which reformulates history in such a way as to render it acceptable to the collective conscience and preclude all doubt as to guilt of the scapegoat.

Obviously, prohibitions, rites, and myths do not always succeed in channeling violence. Real crises regularly crop up, and they require real scapegoats. But more complex prohibitions, rites, and myths are then developed to banish the violence once more. In this fashion, both human consciousness grows, and the complexity of rules, customs, behaviors, and reflections on the art of living. All this makes up what we are accustomed to call human culture.

From crisis to crisis, things improve. The less violence, the more learning and culture. In this sense religious progress is basic, for, as we have seen, violence and the sacred are profoundly interrelated. The day there is a channeling of the human instinct for imitation *without the denouement demanding the sacrifice of a scapegoat,* a giant step will have been taken. Great progress will have been made. To my view, all progress must gradually yield up the biblical conception of life and religion. This conception presents a new revelation of God and a new visualization of the solutions that must be applied to social crises. Theology and conflict are intimately bound up with each other, as we shall see in chapter two. At all events, to eliminate the religious element is to condemn oneself to a total ignorance of the mechanism of conflict.

We may represent the growth of human culture in Figure 2.

Figure 2
Growth of Human Culture

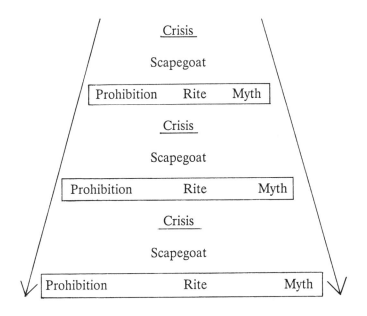

Etc.

Chapter 3

A Nonviolent Rereading of the Bible

All societies are basically erected on the mangled bodies of human victims. *This is the case even materially*, as archaeology knows so well. Excavation of the walls and main gates of ancient cities has often unearthed the mortal remains, the skeletons, of human beings long ago sacrificed in a ritual of consecration of these cities. This is the conception with which the Bible will make a break. Of course, as I have stressed, the break will be gradual. Sacred scripture also contains many traditional religious sacrificial features. Let me cite a few examples:

CAIN AND ABLE (GENESIS 4:1–25)

It is interesting to compare the myth of the founding of Rome with the biblical account of Cain and Abel and the foundation of the city of Cain. First of all, we observe that the antagonists in both instances are siblings—in the case of Romulus and Remus, twins. Siblings, we know, and especially twins, are frequent candidates for a particularly violent brand of competition. The reason for this is precisely that they are so similar. Each is, as it were, the reflex image of the other. What one does, the other imitates, and far more readily than if they had been very differ-

---

Translated by Robert R. Barr.

ent from one another. Their respective fields of existence are not clearly delimited. Everything between them is confused, mixed together, as if in one undifferentiated mass. Such indifferentiation always begets violence, for there is no barrier to mutual imitation. And we have seen that imitation is the invasion of another's field of existence. To imitate is to attempt to gain possession of what belongs to another, and to be what that other is. And so it comes about that siblings, with their minimal natural differentiation and hence maximal candidacy for mutual imitation, can pass from the most intimate friendship to the most intense rivalry. Literature abounds with sibling enemies. Neither they nor public opinion around them at first see any reason for drawing a line of demarcation between them. Then the one oppresses the other. And war breaks out.

We know the legend of the founding of Rome. Romulus traces the limits of the future city with his plow. Remus ignores the implied restriction and transgresses the boundary. He invades his sibling's arena of activity! And Romulus slays him on the spot, immolating him to the gods of the city. And indeed, for a city, a society, or any other human group to exist, there must be a respect for the rules, for the limits or boundaries, that guarantee its existence. No one can transgress those limits with impunity. Otherwise there will never be a group with its own personality. Romulus's act puts an end to the initial confusion prevailing between the brothers—the indifferentiation that had generated such conflict. And of this brutally established differentiation is born a new community: Rome.

In the Roman myth, as handed down by tradition, Romulus is completely justified in his act. No one ascribes the slightest guilt to him. No one accuses him of any violence.

In the biblical myth, the case is altogether different. We perceive a new orientation in the creation of history, amid conventional structures of myth clearly present.

Two rivals and mutual models are opposed, Cain and Abel:

Abel became a keeper of flocks, and Cain a tiller of the soil. In the course of time Cain brought an offering to the Lord God from the fruit of the soil; Abel, for his part, brought one of the firstlings of his flock [Gen. 4:2-4].

Thus the siblings engage in imitation:

> The Lord looked with favor on Abel and his offering, but
> on Cain and his offering he did not. Cain greatly resented
> this and was crestfallen [Gen. 4:4-5].

Conflict arises:

> So the Lord said to Cain: "Why are you so resentful and
> crestfallen? If you do well, you can hold up your head; but
> if not, sin is a demon lurking at the door; his urge is toward
> you, yet you can be his master" [Gen. 4:6-7].

And we have an admirable portrayal of the antagonistic rivalry that seizes Cain—a penetrating definition of mechanisms
of violence presented as all but irresistible.

> Cain said to his brother Abel, "Let us go out in the field."
> When they were in the field, Cain attacked his brother
> Abel and killed him. [Gen. 4:8]

The crisis is resolved by murder. Sacrificial logic has taken
over: in order to emerge from a crisis, someone must be killed.

> Cain said to the Lord: "My punishment is too great to
> bear. . . . I must avoid your presence and become a restless
> wanderer on the earth, anyone may kill me at sight." "Not
> so!" the Lord said to him. "If anyone kills Cain, Cain shall
> be avenged sevenfold." So the Lord put a mark on Cain,
> lest anyone kill him at sight [Gen. 4:13-16].

Cain is protected by a prohibition, lest the rivalry and violence
spread any further. Again we have the concern of traditional
religion (the religion of scapegoat and human sacrifice) to erect
a barrier of myth, rite, and prohibition to the infectious spread
of violence.

> Cain had relations with his wife, and she conceived and
> bore Enoch. Cain also became the founder of a city. . . .

Adah gave birth to Jabal, the ancestor of all who dwell in tents and keep cattle. His brother's name was Jubal; he was the ancestor of all who play the lyre and the pipe. Zillah, on her part, gave birth to Tubalcain, the ancestor of all who forge instruments of bronze and iron [Gen. 4:17-22].

And we have the civil construction industry, the invention of musical instruments, and the creation of metallurgy.

Biblical Myth and Roman Myth

The two myths we have just examined are very different. Cain is presented in the Bible as a simple murderer—who, however, is preserved from the cycle of violence. Neither is his act sacralized, nor is Abel divinized. Cain's mythical foundation of a city and civilization does not exempt him from responsibility for his homicide.

Whereas Romulus and the city he created receive complete approval—along with the act that will make the Roman nation for everlasting a society violent by nature, essence, and origin—Cain and his city are unreservedly condemned. "The Lord then said: 'What have you done! Listen: your brother's blood cries out to me 'from the soil!' " (Gen. 4:10). *The condemnation of the crime outweighs all other considerations in the biblical text. This is the biblical novelty.* The creation of Cain's city is likewise. Thus the Bible enters upon an evolution that will become ever more powerful with the passage of time. In traditional narrative it is the criminal who is innocent and the victim who is guilty. The Bible says just the opposite: society is guilty, the victim is innocent. How often the Judeo-Christian tradition is accused of falsely indicting a humanity that in fact is obviously so "nice" and unblemished! No one seems to wonder whether the Bible might perhaps be entirely right to indict human societies if they are built of the blood of human victims hidden in the holds of the unconscious and the rubble of history.

"Where is your brother?" (Gen. 4:9) comes to be, for the biblical conception, the basic question of all human behavior, individual and societal.

The change in the structure of the myth is basic for the biblical conception of the resolution of conflict. From this moment forward, that structure now *censures* human sacrifices as a solution for social crises. Nor will this be without enormous consequences for the future. If the classic myth is a reformulation of history from a point of departure in the belief of executioners in the guilt (and divinization) of its victims—if that myth incarnates the viewpoint of the reconciled community, which piously holds that the human sacrifice of an expiatory victim has been a legitimate, sacred act *ordained by the deity*—then it is evident that a radical change of opinion in this respect will subvert the traditional religious order, along with its prohibitions, rites and myths.

And indeed, as we have seen, the scapegoat mechanism, and its whole manner of channeling and limiting violence, functions only if the community entertains no slightest doubt of the culpability of the sacrificial victim. Gradually, slowly, a new practice of conflict, a new perception of the true nature of God and religion, will take control of biblical history, and by way of the latter, of human history as well.

JOSEPH AND HIS BROTHERS (GENESIS 37:3–36; 39:7–20)

The story of Joseph and his brothers, one of the most beautiful stores in the bible, is a familiar one. The patriarch Jacob had twelve sons. Two of them, Joseph and Benjamin, were his favorites, because they were the sons of his favorite wife, Rachel. The others were either sons of his other wife, Leah, Rachel's sister, or those of the wives' slaves. Joseph's brothers hated him for the favoritism their father showed him. At the age of seventeen, young Joseph had a dream one night in which he saw himself in a position of superiority with regard to his brothers:

> "Listen to this dream I had. There we were, binding sheaves in the field, when suddenly my sheaf rose to an upright position, and your sheaves formed a ring around my sheaf and bowed down to it." "Are you really going to make yourself king over us?" his brothers asked him. "Or

impose your rule on us?" So they hated him all the more because of his talk about his dreams [Gen. 37:8].

Then Joseph had another dream, and recounted it to his brothers as well:

"I had another dream," he said; "this time, the sun and the moon and eleven stars were bowing down to me." When he also told it to his father, his father reproved him. "What is the meaning of this dream of yours?" he asked. "Can it be that I and your mother and your brothers are to come and bow to the ground before you?" So his brothers were wrought up against him but his father pondered the matter [Gen. 37:8-11]

Here is a typical case of sibling rivalry: one brother is perceived by the others as representing a threat:

One day, Joseph was sent by his father to bring back word of his brothers and their flock. The brothers decided to kill him. They noticed him from a distance, and before he came to them, they plotted to kill him. They said to one another: "Here comes that master dreamer! Come on, let us kill him" [Gen. 37:18-20].

But lest they spill his blood, which of course was theirs as well ("after all, he is our brother, our own flesh" — Gen. 37:27), the brothers decided to sell him to a passing Arab caravan. The Arabs in turn sold him to Potiphar, commandant of the Egyptian pharaoh's personal bodyguard. The brothers deceived old Jacob, the father, by disguising Joseph's disappearance as an accident:

They took Joseph's tunic, and after slaughtering a goat, dipped the tunic in its blood. Then they sent someone to bring the long tunic to their father, with the message: "We found this. See whether it is your son's tunic or not." He recognized it and exclaimed: "My son's tunic! A wild beast has devoured him! Joseph has been torn to pieces!" Then

Jacob rent his clothes, put sackcloth on his loins, and mourned his son many days [Gen. 37:31-34].

In Egypt, Joseph prospered; God walked with him. One day, his master's wife sought to seduce him. Because he refused her advances, she accused him of attempting the very adultery he had spurned.[1] Joseph was put into chains. But even there he was everyone's favorite.

Joseph could interpret dreams, and it was in this capacity that he achieved glory, for the pharaoh, disturbed by nightmares, had need of his services. He interpreted the pharaoh's dreams, and was raised to the position of prime minister of Egypt, for he had foreseen years of plenty, and years of famine, that were to come upon the land. "Could we find another like him," the pharaoh asked his officials, "a man so endowed with the spirit of God?" (Gen. 40:38). Then the pharaoh said to Joseph:

"Since God has made all this known to you . . . you shall be in charge of my palace, and all my people shall dart at your command." . . . With that, the pharaoh took off his signet ring and put it on Joseph's finger [Gen. 41:39–42].

Again a biblical episode conveys a new conception of human relationships and the resolution of conflict.

Then came the years of famine that Joseph had foreseen. Even Jacob and his family, in far-off Canaan, were in the most dire need. Knowing that provisions were to be had in Egypt, the patriarch sent his sons — all but Benjamin, the youngest — to buy there what was needed. And so it happened that, after so many years, ten sons of Jacob, Joseph's brothers, unbeknownst to themselves, stood face to face with the brother they had once wanted to murder. How could they have discerned, in this prestigious gentleman, the pharaoh's prime minister, their victim of so long ago? Joseph recognized *them*, however — as they bowed to the ground before him, just as had the sheaves in the dream he had had once upon a time:

It was Joseph, as governor of the country, who dispensed the rations to all the people. When Joseph's brothers came and knelt down before him with their faces to the ground, he recognized them as soon as he saw them. But he concealed his own identity from them and spoke sternly to them [Gen. 42:6-7].

Joseph will apply an ingenious stratagem, that his innocence may appear in all its brilliance before the eyes of his brothers. He makes use of neither the *prestige of power* nor the *violence of revenge* that lie at his disposition. Neither power nor violence will be of any service in recomposing the family community, long ago destroyed by an attempted murder. Another psychological mechanism, and a most original one, will enter the picture.

The prudent old patriarch Jacob had not sent the darling of the family—his favorite son Benjamin, whose mother was Rachel, Joseph's own mother—along with the older brothers on their journey to Egypt to purchase grain. "It was only Joseph's full brother Benjamin that Jacob did not send with the rest, for he thought some disaster might befall him" (Gen. 42:4).

Sad experience had taught the old man caution. But it is precisely the presence of his full brother that Joseph, now the pharaoh's prime minister, demands of his brothers in return for the foodstuffs they seek to purchase. After a long journey, when the caravan returns with the lad, Joseph delivers the wheat to his family, who still fail to recognize him. But then he sets a trap, so as to be able to accuse Benjamin of theft. He secretly instructs his head steward to conceal his own silver drinking cup in Benjamin's bag before the brothers depart once more for Canaan:

At daybreak the men and their donkeys were sent off. They had not gone far out of the city when Joseph said to his head steward: "Go at once after the men! When you overtake them, say to them, 'Why did you repay good with evil? Why did you steal the silver goblet from me? It is the very one from which my master drinks and which he uses for divination. What you have done is wrong.' " When the steward overtook them and repeated these words to them, they remonstrated with him: "How can my lord say such things? Far be it from your servants to do such a thing!

We even brought back to you from the land of Canaan the money that we found in the mouths of our bags. Why, then, would we steal silver or gold from your master's house? If any of your servants is found to have the goblet, he shall die, and as for the rest of us, we shall become my lord's slaves." But he replied, "Even though it ought to be as you propose, only the one who is found to have it shall become my slave, and the rest of you shall be exonerated." Then each of them eagerly lowered his bag to the ground and opened it, and when a search was made, starting with the oldest and ending with the youngest, the goblet turned up in Benjamin's bag. At this, they tore their clothes. Then, when each man had reloaded his donkey, they returned to the city.

As Judah and his brothers reentered Joseph's house, he was still there; so they flung themselves on the ground before him. "How could you do such a thing?" Joseph asked them. "You should have known that such a man as I could discover by divination what happened." Judah replied: "What can we say to my lord? How can we plead or how try to prove our innocence? God has uncovered your servants' guilt. Here we are, then, the slaves of my lord — the rest of us no less than the one in whose possession the goblet was found." "Far be it from me to act thus!" said Joseph. "Only the one in whose possession the goblet was found shall become my slave; the rest of you may go back safe and sound to your father" [Gen. 44:3-17].

By this time the brothers no longer have recourse to the sacrifice of the youngest of their number for the sake of their own deliverance. All evidence is against the victim. The "stolen" goblet has been found among his effects. The penalty to be inflicted seems lenient in the circumstances: Benjamin will become Joseph's slave. The plot has been most ingeniously laid and executed. Benjamin will be sacrificed as a scapegoat. Then suddenly the unexpected occurs, and the deadly machinery collapses. Judah, Benjamin's eldest brother, offers himself as victim in his place:

Judah then stepped up to [Joseph] and said: "I beg you, my lord, let your servant speak earnestly to my lord, and do not become angry with your servant. . . . For your servant my father said to us, 'As you know, my wife bore me two sons. One of them, however, disappeared, and I had to conclude that he must have been torn to pieces by wild beasts. . . . If you now take this one away from me too, and some disaster befalls him. . . .'

"If then the boy is not with us when I go back to your servant my father, whose very life is bound up with his, he will die. . . . Besides, I, your servant, got the boy from his father by going surety for him, saying, 'If I fail to bring him back to you, father, you can hold it against me forever.' Let me, your servant, therefore, remain in place of the boy as the salve of my lord, and let the boy go back with his brothers. . . . I could not bear to see the anguish that would overcome my father."

Joseph could no longer control himself in the presence of all his attendants, so he cried out: "Have everyone withdraw from me!" Thus no one else was about when he made himself known to his brothers. . . . "I am Joseph," he said to his brothers. "Is my father still in good health?" But his brothers made him no answer, so dumbfounded were they at him. . . .

"I am your brother Joseph, whom you once sold into Egypt. But now do not be distressed, and do not reproach yourselves for having sold me here. It was really for the sake of saving lives that God sent me here ahead of you. . . .

"Tell my father about my high position in Egypt and what you have seen. But hurry and bring my father down here." There upon he flung himself on the neck of his brother Benjamin and wept, and Benjamin wept in his arms. Joseph then kissed all his brothers, crying over each of them; and only then were his brothers able to talk with him [Gen. 44:18–45:15].

How shall we analyze this moving, so very human, biblical narrative? Precisely: it is human, and not mythic. We recognize the classic mythic structure, but that structure is reorientated in an altogether new direction.

Joseph is the cause of disorder and perturbation in the group with his dreams of grandeur. Then the group seeks to make away with him, disguising his disappearance in such a way as to make it acceptable.

Once more the Bible takes side with the victim. The victim escapes death (rejection of human sacrifice as the solution for conflicts) and begins to prosper.[2] The victim will figure at the center of the reconciliation process. That is, the relations between the persecuting, murderous community and the victim are reversed. It is no longer the violent behavior of the community that brings peace. It is the shrewdness and purity of the victim that will finally and completely uproot the violence from the midst of this sibling group.

After all, in order to achieve reconciliation, Joseph must use not only purity (not taking revenge, not utilizing the prestige of his power in order to "force" his brothers' contrition), but also shrewdness. He will "enact" the odious nature of all human sacrifice, and most dramatically, by seeming to cause Benjamin to fall under the threat of punishment by way of example. Joseph produces a true psychodrama. The brothers can no longer bear the thought of having to live with another family murder, which, to boot, would be the death of their aged father. By way of the tragedy of Benjamin, it is Joseph's own tragedy—and innocence—that he causes to flash forth so resplendently in the eyes of his brothers. It is not enough to forgive. The brothers must feel in their flesh what it is to be a scapegoat (through the person of Benjamin) in order definitively to reject the sacrificial logic.

It is likewise interesting to note, for the first time in the Bible, the appearance of the "lamb of God"—someone who, in freedom and innocence, guilty neither in his own conscience nor in the eyes of public opinion, offers his life in exchange for that of the accused. Judah offers himself in Benjamin's stead. Everyone knows Judah is innocent. Not even appearances are against him. He is free to return home. And yet he offers himself as victim in exchange for Benjamin, to save both Benjamin and the father of all the brothers—foreshadowing the attitude of Christ, who declares in Saint John:

The father loves me for this: that I lay down my life to take it up again. No one takes it from me; I lay it down freely. I have power to lay it down, and I have power to take it up again. This command I received from my Father [John 10:17-18].

Christ could have escaped the danger that threatened him. Instead, he offers his life in order to save others.

Finally, let us note that Joseph, contrary to what occurs in the classic myths, is not sacralized or divinized. We have seen that in the classic myths, the sacrificed hero, after having been the object of hatred, becomes the quasi-divine source of blessing. In the present account, Joseph appears merely as a human being happy to make peace with his brothers. It is the loving attitude of Judah, concerned for his youngest brother and for the life of his father, that causes Joseph to overflow with emotion. Joseph perceives that only love dwells in this group now: neither fear of the powerful (Joseph), nor sacrificial violence, has inspired Judah's conduct.

MOSES AND THE EXODUS

In the exodus, it is the entire Hebrew people who assumes the role of the expiatory victim, which classically would be sacrificed at the hands of the dominant, in this case Egyptian, society.

We note that, in a first phase, the Hebrew people rejects the early Moses—the Moses who girds himself in violence and kills the Egyptian guard who has struck one of his Hebrew brothers. The leader who attracts violence is feared: "Who has appointed you ruler and judge over us? Are you thinking of killing me as you killed the Egyptian?" (Exod. 2:14). Moses grew afraid, and fled. This is not the way to the people's liberation and departure from Egypt. Genuine liberation does not consist in taking freedom by storm, by a frontal assault. Genuine liberation occurs when agitation and disturbance become so annoying that the dominant society itself is led to rid itself of the trouble-makers, expel those who claim their freedom. The pharaoh finally begged the Hebrews to leave his land: "Pharaoh summoned Moses and

Aaron and said, 'Leave my people at once, you and the Israelites with you!' " (Exod. 12:31).

In other words, it was Moses himself who provoked the sacrificial crisis that would agitate Egypt. By his behavior, and by the behavior of his people, he brought upon himself persecution (expulsion), just as if he had sought to be the scapegoat whose sacrifice would return peace to Egypt. The plagues that devastated the land of Egypt mean, at the least, that the presence of Israel had become unbearable for the dominating society. It was Israel itself that had truly become a plague. How did Moses manage to provoke such a serious social crisis, to the point that the pharaoh preferred to expel the Hebrew people rather than keeping them in captivity? We do not know. Was it by way of a popular war? History does not tell us. We know that the Hebrew people was insignificant for the giant that was Egypt. Events have been recorded from the viewpoint of Israel, so that phenomena that were doubtless only incidental in the eyes of the Egyptian power have been exaggerated for the purpose of conveying the underlying point: that the Hebrew people provoked its own expulsion.

What is important for us in this analysis is not this series of historical concerns, but the structure of the narrative. We observe the extraordinary fact that the logic of the classic myth is shattered. The expelled, the sacrificed, are the source of new life, a new community, when one would have expected them to be simply incriminated and annihilated.

Ought not the poor to behave in the same way? Ought not the poor to win their freedom by way of their expulsion? Why should they contaminate themselves with the violence of their oppressors by adopting the sacrificial logic, the oppressors' own violent way of reestablishing peace? Let them simply refuse to cooperate with them, whether politically or economically, ideologically or morally. Boycott. Disobey. Reject their ideological customs in favor of an authentic worship of the one true God:

> After that, Moses and Aaron went to the pharaoh and said, "Thus says the Lord, the God of Israel: Let my people go, that they may celebrate a feast to me in the desert: [Exod. 5:1; cf. 7:26; 8:4, etc.].

Their radical refusal to conform to the worship of false values continually causes the Hebrews of today, the poor of every kind, the true adorers of the Lord of history, to be expelled from the society in which they have been immersed and thus to create a new society. In a slum, for example, we discern tokens of this new society in the real common ownership of land. The poor need only radicalize, systematize, and organize this boycott of the oppressor.

We do not thereby deny the persistence of many sacrificial traits in the exodus narrative. The avenging angel wreaks his horror, slaughtering all the firstborn of this land of Egypt (Exod. 11). The chosen people, victim, though they be, are in the grip of a genuine punitive mentality. Victim and executioner are one. We are still very far from the gospel. What is important to observe, once again, is the redirection of history: the Bible's persistence in seeing history from the point of view of the (innocent) victim: the rejected, the expelled, the sacrificed, bear the seed of a new social order, a new creation filled with life. Already the scriptures foreshadow the evangelical "blest are you poor; the reign of God is yours" (Luke 6:20).

Clearly, if the mechanism of the scapegoat is thus subjected to a total boycott, and radically subverted, another psychological mechanism will have to be found for the expulsion of violence from societies in crisis and for the restoration of peace.

LEVITICUS

An interesting text in Leviticus marks a new stage in Israel's evolution toward a new conception of the control of violence:

> Aaron shall bring forward the live goat. Laying both hands on its head, he shall confess over it all the sinful faults and transgressions of the Israelites, and so put them on the goat's head. He shall then have it led into the desert by an attendant. Since the goat is to carry off their iniquities to an isolated region, it must be sent away into the desert [Lev. 16:20 – 22].

Here we have the classic ritual transference. To avoid a human sacrifice, recourse is had to an animal sacrifice. The crisis is celebrated in liturgy, lest it occur in reality. As we have seen, however, the commemoration of a crisis demands a sacrificial outcome and resolution—in the present case, an animal sacrifice. But let us be under no illusions: behind the sacrifice of nonhuman living beings lurks the ongoing possibility of a human sacrifice. Many peoples reached the stage of the substitution of animal sacrifice for human sacrifice. The Hebrew nation was not alone in this. Substitution, however, is not overthrow. And once more the Bible shows its originality: the prophets of Israel will continually cast suspicion on animal sacrifice, for they discern the violent sacrificial logic upon which it rests. It is the mentality itself, not just the material act, that they seek to uproot.

THE LAW AND THE PROPHETS

The texts of the prophets are too abundant, and too clear, for their antisacrificial intent to be missed.

Micah 6:6—18

The prophet shows that animal sacrifice is simply child sacrifice, disguised:

> With what shall I come before the Lord,
>   and bow before God most high?
> Shall I come before him with holocausts,
>   with calves a year old?
> Will the Lord be pleased with thousands of rams,
>   with myriad streams of oil?
> Shall I give my first-born for my crime,
>   the fruit of my body for the sin of my soul?
> You have been told, O man, what is good,
>   and what the Lord requires of you:
>   Only to do right and to love goodness,
>   and to walk humbly with your god.

The burden of the prophets' warning is ever the same: legal rites, ceremonies, worship, are of little importance. What is important is that you not fight among yourselves — that you not become sibling enemies![3]

Isaiah 1:11–17

> What care I for the number of your sacrifices?
>> says the Lord.
> I have had enough of whole-burnt rams
>> and fat of fatlings;
> In the blood of calves, lambs, and goats
>> I find no pleasure. . . .
> Bring no more worthless offerings. . . .
> When you spread out your hands,
>> I close my eyes to you;
> Though you pray the more,
>> I will not listen.
> Your hands are full of blood!
>> Wash yourselves clean!
> Put away your misdeeds from before my eyes;
>> cease doing evil; learn to do good,
> Make justice your aim: redress the wronged,
>> hear the orphan's plea, defend the widow.

Hosea 6:6

The principle of sacrifice is rejected. Hosea comes very close to proclaiming a sincere conversion of heart as the only viable sacrifice:

> For it is love that I desire, not sacrifice,
>> and knowledge of God rather than holocausts.

Indeed the "liturgical temptation" is among the very subtlest of temptations, for it substitutes rite for reality. But one reality alone pacifies God (and the community that ought to be in the image and likeness of God). That reality is the sincere conversion of the heart, a praxis of peace.

Psalm 51

We see it in the psalms. For example, hear this "psalm of David, when Nathan the prophet came to him after his sin with Bathsheba" and the death of her husband Uriah, which David had contrived:

> Have mercy on me, O God, in your goodness;
>> in the greatness of your compassion wipe out my offense. . . .
> Behold, you are pleased with sincerity of heart. . . .
> For you are not pleased with sacrifices;
>> should I offer a holocaust, you would not accept it.
> My sacrifice, O God, is a contrite spirit;
>> a heart contrite and humbled, O God, you will not spurn [vv. 1–19].

Amos 5:21–24

> I hate, I spurn your feasts,
>> I take no pleasure in your solemnities.
> Your cereal offerings I will not accept,
>> nor consider your stall-fed peace offerings. . . .
> But if you would offer me holocausts,
>> then let justice surge like water,
>> and goodness like an unfailing stream.

Jeremiah 7:4–11

Jeremiah anticipates Jesus' assault on the temple, central locus of Israel's worship and symbol of a sacrificial religion:

> Put not your trust in the deceitful words: "This is the temple of the Lord! The temple of the Lord! The temple of the Lord!" Only if you thoroughly reform your ways and your deeds; if each of you deals justly with his neighbor; if you no longer oppress the resident alien, the orphan,

and the widow; if you no longer shed innocent blood in this place, or follow strange gods to your own harm, will I remain with you in this place, in the land which I gave your fathers long ago and forever. But here you are, putting your trust in deceitful words to your own loss! Are you to steal and murder, commit adultery and perjury, burn incense to Baal, go after strange gods that you know not, and yet come to stand before me in this house which bears my name, and say: "We are safe; we can commit all these abominations again"? Has this house which bears my name become in your eyes a den of thieves?

Yahweh refuses to renew his covenant with a people that substitutes liturgy for righteousness.

The prophets mince no words, then, in their condemnation of sacrificial rite. The scapegoat mechanism, ritual or real, will have to be rejected. But now a serious problem arises. In case of serious, violent social crisis, how will society be able to cope?

We must make every effort to grasp all the consequences of the prophets' rejection of human sacrifice as part of the social relationship. That rejection is tantamount to the assertion that *no human being, not even the most wicked, is totally responsible for the violence of the group.* The violence is the community's as well. To cast the whole blame on one individual, even a guilty one, is a mystification, and will not eliminate the evil. To slay Hitler or Somoza is not enough! No human being, whatever the degree of his or her responsibility for the prevailing evil, may be sacrificed for the good of all as if that individual were the only one responsible. We must ever recall that the "person responsible" is responsible only in a qualified way, only "in moderation." The community must maintain a consciousness of its own guilt—the blame that lies with itself.

But in this case, if we accept René Girard's original hypothesis, peace will never return, for there will be no way to discharge responsibility for violence on anyone. Neither will the actual cause of the disturbance of public order be found. Thus the group will not be calmed. It will continue to be agitated, afflicted, and violent.

The answer to this difficulty is available only through a religious revolution, beginning with Abraham and culminating in the gospel. God is not violent. Human sacrifice does not please God. Reconciliation will come by way of some righteous individual who will freely surrender to the strokes and blows of the violent. In this fashion, through the suffering of the innocent, the community will acquire a consciousness of the senseless and hateful nature of its conduct. This time the violence will be definitively uprooted, for this time the entire community will be discovered to be the vehicle of the evil suffered by that same community. Buried violence will be disinterred in all, not just in the outlaw! In other words, the relationship will be inverted.

If this new mechanism is to function, evidently a mediator must be found who is innocent of any complicity with violence: someone altogether pure and righteous. Only such a one will be able to disclose the violence that resides within the entire community as such, and call forth the contrition of that community. The innocence of an innocent victim must be so clear that the masses of the people will automatically look to the community itself for the cause of this horrible destruction.

The Roman official and soldiers who stood guard at the foot of Jesus' cross confessed: "Clearly this was the Son of God!" (Matt. 27:54). The soldiers and the people who participated in the execution of Joan of Arc returned to their homes saying, "We have burned a saint!" The possibility of another kind of human victim, one who surrenders life freely and brings peace, supposes an act of faith, and not only an act of faith in the basic goodness of the human being—of the whole human being, and of all human beings (capable of acknowledging their violence, despite all, and of repenting)—but, to resume the language of the initial hypothesis, an act of faith in the capacity of at least one righteous individual (and that one's disciples) voluntarily to limit the imitation of appropriation and antagonism: to refuse to be drawn into the (violent) game of such as could wish to gain control of an object whose owner would thereupon attempt to regain it in the same manner (by way of an act of revenge); to refuse to imitate the violence of the one who would wish to gain control of my life. Jesus means nothing else in his celebrated, radical declaration: "When a person strikes you on the right cheek, turn and offer him the other" — rejection of the imitation of antagonism. "If anyone wants to go to law over your shirt, hand him your coat as well" — rejection of the imitation of appropriation (Matt. 5:39–40).

The new, innocent mediator is likewise proclaimed by the prophets. In freely embracing the path of suffering, this mediator reveals to the community its own wickedness, and thus achieves a far more radical reconciliation than could ever have been attained through the mechanism of the scapegoat.

JOB

What is the real meaning of the story of Job? Is Job only the tale of a poor unfortunate reduced to extreme misery, and bawling his innocence at the top of his lungs? Job's three companions come to share his pain and console him. Despite their good intentions, however, they are the allies of evil, for they seek at any cost to have Job don the mask of the scapegoat, and declare himself guilty, deserving of punishment. Again we recognize the age-old logic of sacrificial justice, a logic that will never accept a scapegoat's innocence:

What is a man that he should be blameless. . .
If in his holy ones God places no confidence,
        and if the heavens are not clean in his sight,
How much less so is the abominable, the corrupt:
        who drinks in iniquity like water?
                [Job 15:14-15].

Job must neither resign himself, then, nor despise the lessons of the Lord, till God have mercy on him. Job's friends slay him all over again. They see his misfortune, and tell him that it is his own fault. But Job refuses to assume this scapegoat role, and shouts his innocence to the heavens. He answers his friends:

I have heard this sort of thing many times.
        Wearisome comforters are you all!
Is there no end to windy words? [Job 16:2-3].

Eventually Job goes so far as to attack God himself as conceptualized in the theology of the day:

> As God lives, who withholds my deserts,
> > the Almighty, who has made bitter my soul,
> So long as I still have life in me. . . .
> My lips shall not speak falsehood,
> > nor my tongue utter deceit!
> Far be it from me to account you right:
> > till I die iI will not renounce my innocence
> > > [Job 27:2-4].

What a pathetic picture! What a lonely, isolated, abandoned individual—rejecting the mask of the criminal, which even his best friends want him to wear! As we see once more, in order to execute anyone, we must first demoralize and calumniate that person. Job is the first great biblical figure to utter a scream of protest against this sacrificial procedure. But behind Job stand the millions of innocent men and women who, over the course of the centuries, have been calumniated and sacrificed in order to reestablish law and order. Job lends them his voice, that they may proclaim their innocence.

But we are still only at midpoint of the evolution under consideration. We have not yet reached the nonviolent God of the gospel. True, God admits the justice of Job's cause (a novelty indeed!):

> The Lord said to Eliphaz the Temanite, "I am angry with you and with your two friends; for you have not spoken rightly concerning me, as has my servant Job" [Job 42:7].

This last text, then, is public acknowledgment that Job's suffering, like all misfortune, is the work not of God, but of Satan. God does not create death. Human perdition does not please God. This is the great theme of the wisdom literature. However, God does not as yet explain to Job the mysterious wisdom of the Suffering Servant, the persecuted righteous one. Only with the famous text of Isaiah 53 does this revelation begin.

ISAIAH

He grew up like a sapling before [the Lord],
      like a shoot from the parched earth;
There was in him no stately bearing to make us look
      at him,
      nor appearance that would attract us to him.
He was spurned and avoided by men,
      a man of suffering, accustomed to infirmity,
One of those from whom men hide their faces,
      spurned, and we held him in no esteem.
Yet it was our infirmities that he bore,
      our sufferings that he endured,
While we thought of him as stricken,
      as one smitten by God and afflicted.
But he was pierced for our offenses,
      crushed for our sins;
Upon him was the chastisement that makes us whole,
      by his stripes we were healed.
We had all gone astray like sheep,
      each following his own way;
But the Lord laid upon him
      the guilt of us all.

Though he was harshly treated, he submitted
      and opened not his mouth;
Like a lamb led to the slaughter
      or a sheep before the shearers,
      he was silent and opened not his mouth.
Oppressed and condemned, he was taken away,
      and who would have thought any more of his
      destiny?
When he was cut off from the land of the living,
      and smitten for the sin of his people,
A grave was assigned him among the wicked
      and a burial place with evildoers,
Though he had done no wrong
      nor spoken any falsehood.

[But the Lord was pleased to crush him in infirmity]
[Isaiah 53:2-10].

Here is a wealth of elements constituting or reenforcing the evolution we perceive in the Bible toward a new way of making peace:

The savior is scarcely "good looking," or beautiful, for he is laden with the suffering of others (verses 3,5). We find this today in the persons of the poor, deformed indeed by the harsh life they lead in the service of the wealthy.

The victim is consciously recognized and acknowledged by the community as innocent and just. He maintains no complicity with evil (vv. 5, 9): "though he had done no wrong."

The victim freely surrenders. No one takes the victim's life by force: "Though he was harshly treated, he submitted" (v. 7).

Through the suffering of the righteous victim, the community becomes conscious of the evil it harbors in its bosom: "He was pierced for our offenses, crushed for our sins" (v. 5).

By suffering, and by way of the conscientization this suffering provokes, the righteous victim gathers the community once more, for its members "had all gone astray like sheep, each following his own way" (v. 6).

There remains the ambiguous role of God. On the one hand, it is implied that God is not responsible for the evil that crushes the righteous. We thought of him as "one smitten by God and afflicted" (v. 4), but such was not the case: in actuality "he was pierced for our offenses, crushed for our sins" (v. 5). The community, and not God, now appears as the main culprit. And yet we find the typically sacrificial expression, "the Lord laid upon him the guilt of us all" (v. 6); "the Lord was pleased to crush him in infirmity" (v. 10)—a God who enjoys crushing a victim!

The evolution will come to perfection only in the gospel. But till then, how can we overlook a revision, a "reconscientization," of the mechanisms of conflict, and a new, nonviolent conception of God—a new theology—spanning the whole of the Old Testament?

To be sure, the biblical myths are infected with a spirit that goes against their grain. And yet they subsist. Sacrifice is criticized, and yet it continues. The law (with its prohibitions) is simplified, identified with love, and yet it continues in force. And so on. Nevertheless, I hold, a dynamic reading of sacred scripture such as the one we here propose, a reading that utilizes the tool of an extremely interesting anthropological hypothesis, has the capacity to renew our theology of conflict and our corresponding pastoral practice, by way of the substantiation of *a new continuity* between Old and New Testaments on the matter of peace and war.

Chapter 4

The Logic of the Lamb of God

It remains to situate the New Testament in this great evolution. We can do this very rapidly.

According to René Girard, the gospels only mention sacrifice in order to reject it. To the ritualism of the Pharisees, Jesus opposes the antisacrificial pronouncement of Hosea, cited above: "Go and learn the meaning of the words, 'It is mercy I desire and not sacrifice' " (Matt. 9:13; cf. Hos. 6:6).[1] Let us also consider another text:

> If you bring your gift to the altar and there recall that your brother has anything against you, leave your gift at the altar, go first to be reconciled with your brother, and then come and offer your gift [Matt. 5:23-24].

This is no mere moral precept. This is the solemn cancellation of liturgical sacrifice, which cannot substitute for reconciliation. We know the mutual hatred that prevailed among the dominant classes of Israel—the Pharisees, the Herodians, and the high priests. Despite their reciprocal enmity, however, they are all the guardians of the established religious and social "law and order," and it is in their common interest that this law and order

---

Translated by Robert R. Barr.

be maintained. They will have to strike an alliance against any disturber of the peace. Nothing could be more false than to imagine a noncombative nonviolence on the part of Jesus. Quite the contrary, Jesus fairly excoriates the three pillars of traditional religion: the *law*, with its prohibitions, the sacrificial *rite* of the temple, and the entire *mythical* structure of the biblical narratives. That is, he continues and perfects the work of the prophets, drawing the veil from the human sacrifices that traditional religion cloaks in a discourse that renders them tolerable. He demonstrates that, for conflicts to be resolved, no one, nothing, need be sacrificed. Finally, he completes theology, showing that God is nonviolent, that God has no taste for sacrifice, disease, or anything at all in the way of pestilence, starvation, storm, and so on—any of the forces of death that lay waste humanity.

All of Jesus' practical comportment is directed against these things, and proves that God is no friend of death. Jesus' practice is one of *healing* and the alleviation of human suffering, not punishment. This fight costs him his life. And he is very conscious that his conception of God and human life will lead him to this mortal outcome. Indeed he freely surrenders himself to that outcome. We may say in all truth that Jesus *strives with might and main against all human sacrifice.* His enemies, before murdering him, seek to invest him with the cloak of the scapegoat, in order to reestablish the sacrificial order and prevent its subversion. They do everything they can to present Jesus to the people as a politically and religiously dangerous individual, and as such deserving of death. In the meantime, the community of the disciples, despite their weakness, manage to pierce the diabolical scheme (the devil, who has been a liar and a murderer "from the beginning"—John 8:43-44) and show forth in all its brilliance the innocence of the Master who from this moment forward will never cease to have supporters, disciples, followers who will continue the work he has begun: the unmasking of this crime and its replacement with love.

This was Jesus' path. Let us examine that path more closely.

THE LAW AND ITS PROHIBITIONS

The Sabbath

It happened that he was walking through standing grain on the Sabbath, and his disciples began to pull off heads

of grain as they went along. At this the Pharisees pro-
tested: "Look! Why do they do a thing not permitted on
the Sabbath?" He said to them: "Have you never read
what David did when he was in need and he and his men
were hungry? How he entered God's house in the days of
Abiathar the high priest and ate the holy bread, which only
the priests were permitted to eat? He even gave it to his
men." Then he said to them, "The Sabbath was made for
humankind, not humankind for the Sabbath" [Mark 2:23-
27; cf. Matt. 12:1-8; Luke 6:1-5].

Matthew and Luke add that the reason why Jesus' disciples
were "harvesting" grain—pulling a few ears of wheat off the
stalk!—on the Sabbath day was simply that they were hungry,
and needed to eat. The Sabbath prohibition against performing
work on the Lord's day had become in fact a taboo! This was
the height of the absurd. One was not allowed even to heal a
diseased person on the Sabbath!

He returned to the synagogue where there was a man
whose hand was shriveled up. They kept an eye on Jesus
to see whether he would heal him on the Sabbath, hoping
to be able to bring an accusation against him. He addressed
the man with the shriveled hand: "Stand up here in front!"
Then he said to them: "Is it permitted to do a good deed
on the Sabbath—or an evil one? To preserve life—or destroy it?" At this they remained silent. He looked around
at them with anger, for he was deeply grieved that they
had closed their minds against him. Then he said to the
man, "Stretch out your hand." The man did so and his
hand was perfectly restored [Mark 3:1-5].

"The Sabbath was made for humankind, and not humankind
for the Sabbath." We are hearing some of the most revolutionary
words of the gospel! If law does no human service, it should be
disobeyed! We, too, Jesus' disciples of today, ought to do as did
the disciples of that time. We should make inroads into fields
and plantations of every kind, of forest and farm, of brick and
concrete, wherever customs and decrees prevent persons from

living—even if by so doing it were to be necessary to disobey the law. For the law is not an absolute, and may never be legitimately protected by a taboo.

Jesus' battle against the prohibitions that are an obstacle to life bring him down to death. "When the Pharisees went outside, they immediately began to plot with the Herodians how they might destroy him" (Mark 3:6). As we have noted, in the normal course of things the Herodians and the Pharisees were mortal enemies. But this is a special case. And they eagerly strike an alliance against their common enemy.

Finally, the antisacrificial note is far from absent from Jesus' struggle. In the Matthean version of the episode of the ears of grain (Matt. 12:1-8), Jesus says: "If you understood the meaning of the text, 'It is mercy I desire and not sacrifice,' you would not have condemned these innocent men" (Matt. 12:7, referring to Hos. 6:6).

The Temple

> When they reached Jerusalem he entered the temple precincts and began to drive out those who were engaged in buying and selling. He overturned the money-changers' tables and the stalls of the men selling doves. ... Then he began to teach them: "Does not scripture have it, *'My house shall be called a house of prayer for all peoples'—?* but you have turned it into a den of thieves" [Mark 11:15-17].

This is surely a vigorous attitude, not only because Jesus is so energetic in his defiance of the authorities, but especially because he casts doubt on the function now exercised by the temple. The sacrifices performed there, like all the business dealing surrounding them, are a far cry from the authentic prayer of his Father's desire.

Jesus' critical attitude vis-á-vis the prevailing sacrificial rite is confirmed over and over again in the gospel. And Jesus knows perfectly well that in criticizing it he is touching on a basic element in the religious equilibrium of the nation—indeed, a basic element in the religiousness of humanity itself.

Jesus is not rash. He takes care not to unleash the storm

before its hour. In Mark 1:40-45 he heals a leper, but strictly charges him to respect traditional religious customs: " 'Not a word to anyone, now,' he said. 'Go off and present yourself to the priest and offer for your cure what Moses prescribed' " (Mark 1:43-44). But the leper, healed of his disease and beside himself with joy, ignores the Master's request. He publishes the news, and now "it was no longer possible for Jesus to enter a town openly. He stayed in desert places," to avoid, or provoke no further, the wrath of the religious authorities. "Yet people kept coming to him from all sides" (Mark 1:45).

Jesus asks: "Go off and present yourself to the priest," and the leper fails to do so. Nor does he "offer for his cure what Moses prescribed" — a sacrificial offering. The temple system begins to be abandoned. Judaism's essential rite is under attack. The authorities perceive the danger, and once more their reaction is: death to such a one! "The chief priests and the scribes heard of this and began to look for a way to destroy him. . . . The whole crowd was under the spell of his teaching" (Mark 11:18).

No sacrifice, no sacrificial ritual, will suffice to save or heal, Jesus is saying.

THE ROLE OF MURDER IN THE FOUNDATION OF SOCIETY

In ancient times these parallel passages went by the name of the "Cursing of the Pharisees." Actually they constitute a much more far-reaching condemnation. Their object comprises all religious persons who, however filled with zeal for God, are so caught up in some lie dear to their hearts that they no longer perceive the extent to which their religion disguises, dissembles, justifies the violence at the root of every human community. Indeed, we must say that all humanity stands condemned here — even atheistic humanity, for it, too, kills in order to reestablish peace, and then justifies this slaughter with rationalizations every bit as hypocritical as those brought forward by religious authorities. Perhaps the most terrible part of this passage is its conclusion, whether in the Matthean or the Lukan version:

Vipers' nest! Brood of serpents! How can you escape condemnation to Gehenna? . . . I shall send you prophets and
wise men and scribes. Some you will kill and crucify, others
you will flog in your synagogues and hunt down from city
to city; until retribution overtakes you for all the blood of
the just ones shed on earth, from the blood of holy Abel
to the blood of Zechariah son of Barachiah, whom you
murdered between the temple building and the altar
[Matt. 23:33-36; cf. Luke 11:39-52].

The Matthean text has a universal dimension. Jesus invokes
the blood of all the just ever spilled out upon the earth, without
specifying Israel as the sole culprit in this horrible bloodshed.
And Luke adds explicitly that this blood is all the blood "shed
since the foundation of the world" (Luke 11:50). Clearly, Abel's
murder here is a symbolic indictment of *all* human civilizations.
The importance of Abel's murder in the Bible, and of the gospel
reference to that murder, is, first of all, that this is the first
biblical account of the violent death of one human being at the
hands of another. And secondly, this same account unveils, for
the first time, the heinous role of murder in the foundation of
human communities. We need only recall what has been said
above concerning the foundation of the city of Cain.

Jesus completes this revelation. He defines his mission, in
particular his habit of speaking in parables, as springing from
the need to proclaim things hidden from the foundation of the
world (Matt. 13:35).[2] And in John he allows this complaint to
escape his lips:

Why do you not understand what I say?
It is because you cannot bear to hear my word.
The father you spring from is the devil,
and willingly you carry out his wishes.
He brought death to man from the beginning,
and has never based himself on truth;
the truth is not in him.
Lying speech
is his native tongue;
he is a liar and the father of lies [8:43-44].

Satan, lying, and murder; an inseparable trio. To be a child
of Satan is to have lying as one's parent. What lying? Precisely
the lie that consists in *dissembling the foundational murder of
society* — the violence that has reestablished law and order, and
that will gladly kill again, if need be, to keep secret the original
murder. Murder calls forth murder, and the whole chain of
slaughter is the consequence of a lie. The world is steeped in
this concatenation of murder and lie. Satan is the prince of this
world, Saint John repeats.

Jesus and the prophets before him came to work a radical
change in this diabolical order. Jesus knows very well that the
Jews he attacks with such passion in the texts we have cited are
not the direct authors of the death of the prophets, just as Christians have not personally murdered Jesus. Both are the *descendants* of those who slew the prophets — and Jesus (Matt. 23:31).

And these descendants will say: "Had we lived in our fore-
fathers' time, we would not have joined them in shedding the
prophets' blood" (Matt. 23:30).

But our very indictment of our ancestors shows our moral
solidarity with them in the violence of which we accuse them.
Although they disown any personal responsibility for the violence that has murdered the prophets, the descendants of the
original murderers nevertheless do exactly what their forebears
have done — kill in order to remove violence from the community. As long as the community refuses to recognize its responsibility, it will continue its lethal, sacrificial logic, and discharge
its own blame and guilt upon the heads of others.

In Luke's Gospel Jesus expresses all of this in his strikingly
perceptive observation:

Woe to you! You build the tombs of the prophets, but it
was your fathers who murdered them. You show that you
stand behind the deeds of your fathers; they committed
the murders and you erect the tombs [Luke 11:47-48].

In other words, every civilization, every culture, every human
construction is like a tomb. A tomb both hides and honors the
deceased. Now more than ever, the task of Jesus and his disciples is to disinter the human victims who have been sacrificed

in the name of law and order from the foundation of the world.

It is curious to observe that these old Judeo-Christian writings of ours, our sacred scripture, scorned by so many, yield a profoundly subversive reading key for the deciphering of human existence. So many Christians, including revolutionaries, make an altogether conservative reading of the sacred text. They read the Bible with sacrificial eyes. They find, for example, that there can be just wars; and thereby they deprive atheists—who, in their rationalism, regard our religious language with such contempt—of a critical instrument that could expel violence from our midst.

JESUS' THEOLOGY OF CONFLICT

Clearly, the conception of God (theology) and the conception of conflict are deeply bound up with each other. Jesus would never have arrived at his penetrating analysis of society had he not taken account of the theological evolution perceptible in the great prophets. For Jesus, definitively, God is a nonviolent God. Perhaps the capital text here is the following:

> My command to you is: love your enemies, pray for your persecutors. This will prove that you are sons of your heavenly Father, for his sun rises on the bad and the good, he rains on the just and the unjust [Matt. 5:44-45].

God does not solve the problem of human evil by means of a violent elimination of the corrupt. (See also the parable of the weeds, Matt. 13:24-30, where the farmer refuses to uproot the weeds until harvest time.) The sun of God's love shines on just and unjust, good and evil. But this does not mean that God watches impassively and undisturbed at the proliferation of evil and the massacre of the innocent. It means that a new way of waging war has appeared on the face of the earth.

The Bible, as the Reverend Dumas explains, records three ways of making war.[3] The first, and oldest, tells of a God who fights *alongside* the people. The commandment not to kill does not apply to war. On the contrary, God, in the midst of the people, with weapons in hand, is the valiant warrior (Exod.

15:3). God's campaign tent is the ark of the covenant, which is carried into battle alongside the others. God's name par excellence is Yahweh of Armies, the Lord of Hosts (Ps. 24:10; Isa. 17:45). War is a sacred act ordained by God, a *holy war*. But the purpose of war is not the military or nationalistic glory of the people. The purpose of war is fidelity to God. The chosen people are never permitted to surrender their identity as the People of God, either by marriage or by commerce. It is the integrity of the faith that is at stake, and the danger of idolatry. In this conceptualization, God can desert a people's armies if that people is unfaithful—if it commits idolatry—and even fight on the side of its enemies (Josh. 5:13-15; Amos 5:27, etc.).

The notion of a holy war, in which God fights side by side with the people, is demolished with the Babylonian captivity (586 B.C.). Although the people will be restored to the land of promise, and led back from exile, never again will there be a king, an army, or the ark.

Now a second conception of war appears—the *messianic war*, in which God fights for the people single-handed. God is the people's champion. The Messiah will fight for his own, without their physical, material cooperation. After all, it had been precisely Israel's blind faith in its own temporal weapons that in olden times had led to disaster.

From now on, faith is hope, without personal involvement, hope in the personal intervention of Yahweh who, in the last days, will come to save the elect.

In the final battle, victory will be God's, and God will reestablish Jerusalem. All nations will flock to the holy city. The messianic conception of war was the common one in the time of Jesus. It can be summarized as follows:

1. The coming of the liberator, the Messiah, is at hand. The life of the people, of the lowly, is about to be changed altogether.

2. The Messiah will be preceded by his herald, Elijah, come back from heaven. As we know, in the time of Jesus some imagined that John the Baptist was Elijah, as he indeed heralded the coming of the Messiah.

3. Once the Messiah is about to burst upon the scene, evil will form a united front of resistance to the liberator.

4. After a lengthy struggle and many battles, the militia of

evil will be destroyed by the hosts of the Messiah, the prince of peace, who will establish his reign in Jerusalem.

5. And this will be the moment of the last judgment and the resurrection of the dead.

Such were the notions of Palestine's "progressives" at the time of Jesus' ministry. The messianists expected the Lord to come down like a thunderbolt, and snatch the Messiah from the snares of his adversaries. He would take him down from the cross, for example. This is why Jesus' enemies taunted him as he hung helpless on the wood of the cross: "Come down from the cross if you are God's Son! ... So he is the king of Israel! Let's see him come down from that cross and then we will believe in him. He relied on God; let God rescue him now if he wants to" (Matt. 27:40-43).

Jesus would have shared these convictions, and indeed he cried out before he expired: *"Eli, Eli, lama sabachthani?"* — that is, "My God, my God, why hast thou forsaken me?" (Matt. 27:46).

But this phrase is only the first line of Psalm 22, which ends with these words of hope:

> For he has not spurned nor disdained
> > the wretched man in his misery,
> Nor did he turn his face away from him,
> > but when he cried out to him, he heard him
> > > [Ps. 22:25].

There were those standing about who, their minds and hearts steeped in the apocalyptic of the day, responded: "Leave him alone. Let's see whether Elijah comes to his rescue" (Matt. 27:49).

Once more we must be able to distinguish between the essential and the accessory — between appearance and reality. The gospel text is written in a context. It is entirely to be expected that the ideas of the age (the context) should show through the gospel text itself. But what actually is the tissue, the "plot," of the gospel? What does the gospel say? Where is the Word, the authentic expression of the divine intention? We must keep in mind the words and deeds of Jesus *in globo*, the whole warp and woof of the gospel. We must not lend this text with our principle of interpretation precisely the religious mentality against which Jesus struggled his whole life long. The proclamations of the passion (Matt. 16:21-23; Mark 8:31-33; Luke 9:22) show us a Jesus who has his eyes wide open where reality is concerned. He is not the prisoner of the apocalyptic mentality of the time. On the contrary, he scolds Peter severely for entertaining that mentality:

> From then on Jesus [the Messiah] started to indicate to his disciples that he must go to Jerusalem and suffer greatly there at the hands of the elders, the chief priests, and the scribes, and to be put to death, and raised up on the third day. At this Peter took him aside and began to remonstrate with him. "May you be spared, Master! God forbid that any such thing ever happen to you!" Jesus turned on Peter and said, "Get out of my sight, you satan! You are trying to make me trip and fall. You are not judging by God's standards but by human standards" [Matt. 16:21-23].

This text represents, at the least, a messianic conception of the primitive Christian community that was different from the apocalyptic mentality of the rest of Judaism.

There can be no doubt that, with his death on the cross, without a divine rescue like a bolt from the blue to snatch the Messiah from the cross, this second conception of the divine warfare, that of the messianic war, falls to the ground. Now there appears the third manner in which Yahweh wages war. We might call it that of *evangelical warfare*. By way of the spectacle of the suffering of the righteous one, whose innocence clearly appears, the community becomes aware of the odious nature of the violence of the case, and conscious of its own guilt in the matter. This conscientization definitively eliminates the violence, inasmuch as the guilt is now seen to reside in all, and not only in an expiatory victim, a scapegoat. And so the evolution is complete—the development we perceive in so many biblical passages and episodes, in the case of Joseph and Benjamin, the suffering servant of Second Isaiah, and so on. The last sacrificial traits of the Old Testament, the elements of the scapegoat logic residual in the most advanced of the Old Testament texts, now disappear. God takes no pleasure in crushing and wounding the servant (Isa. 53:6, 10). The culprits in the murder of the righteous are the members of the community, not God. And this is the Old Testament prophecy selected by the evangelist John as the final line of his account of Christ's passion: "They shall look on him whom they have pierced" (John 19:37; cf. Zech. 12:10).

Luke, too, notes the crowd's repentance:

The centurion, upon seeing what had happened, gave glory to God by saying, "Surely this was an innocent man." When the crowd which had assembled for this spectacle saw what had happened, they went home beating their breasts [Luke 23:47; cf. Matt. 27:45, 50; Mark 15:39].

The sacrificial schema lies in smithereens. The logic of the gospel holds full sway.

INCRIMINATED COMMUNITY VS. INNOCENT LAMB OF GOD

The death of the righteous one has a curious power. It penetrates the noblest fibers of the human heart. It moves the multitude. It summons forth a far mightier unity than that conjured up by the mimetic imitation of the enemy and the murderous alliance of all against one. It bestows an immeasurably greater security than the safety of weaponry. But for this it is necessary that the community of disciples of the Just One have the courage to profess, at the price of their lives if need be, their Master's innocence. It is perfectly clearer that Jesus' enemies attempted to destroy him morally and make of him a classic scapegoat. They sought to destroy him politically by accusing him of being the enemy of the reigning Caesar. They tried to destroy him religiously by accusing him of blaspheming and seeking to destroy the temple. And they all but succeeded in persuading the people of their dishonest accusations. How discouraged, for example, were the anonymous disciples of the road to Emmaus! What respect they continued to maintain for "our chief priests and leaders" (Luke 24:20)!

But the apostolic community managed to gather its courage, pierce through the diabolical scheme, and see to it that Jesus' innocence was recognized. This will be the burden of Peter's postresurrection discourses, which are among the oldest texts of the New Testament, and the best examples we have of the primitive preaching:

> The God of Abraham, of Isaac, and of Jacob, the God of our fathers, has glorified his Servant Jesus, whom you handed over and disowned in Pilate's presence when Pilate was ready to release him. You disowned the Holy and Just one and preferred instead to be granted the release of a murderer [Acts 3:13-14].

> "Therefore let the whole house of Israel know beyond any doubt that God has made both Lord and Messiah this Jesus whom you crucified."
> When they had heard this, they were deeply shaken. They asked Peter and the other apostles, "What are we to do, brothers?" [Acts 2:36-37].

René Girard is concerned to stress what a brief time span determines whether a nonviolent war will be lost or won:

> There is no middle position between killing and being killed. Those who think that such a statement is exaggeratedly pessimistic fail to perceive that the relative peace enjoyed by [the nonviolent activist after a partial victory] is always due to the violence [of the sacrificial system]. If they do not die, then, it is because they maintain some degree of complicity with the violence [of law and order]. A completely innocent, pure person, a stranger to violence, will necessarily become its victim.[4]

And he adds:

The dilemma is the following. Either you set violence against violence, and automatically join its game, or you do not oppose it and immediately it stops your mouth. The regime of violence is so constituted that its revelation is impossible. The truth that provokes violence cannot pitch its tent in the community. It is necessarily expelled. It might perhaps be heard at the very moment it is expelled, at the precise instant at which it refuses to oppose violence with violence. At that moment, becoming victim, in the short space of time that precedes its crushing, is the moment it must reach our ears—the very moment when violence will stop its mouth. That truth must say enough to unmask the unjust order, and thus throw open the floodgates of violence upon its own head, but it must maintain a sufficiently lucid testimony to recount the deed, just as it has occurred, without transforming it.[5]

This shrewdness, this purity, of the nonviolent struggle is the whole secret of evangelical war.

And our paradoxical conclusion will be that, in a war, if anyone must die, it must be the righteous one, not the monster. But this must occur under the conditions that we have set forth: that his disciples testify to his innocence.

Chapter 5

Mechanisms of Collective Violence[1]

As is obvious, the nature of collective conflict has changed in the second half of our century. Of old, fifty or a thousand individuals could be killed by such-and-such a number of persons armed with such-and-such a number of weapons. Today, a much smaller number of persons can kill a far greater number of the adversary. The conditions of conflict have changed, and simple military logic dissuades the poor from ever taking the field when the adversary enjoys overwhelming superiority in lethal arms. Other means of combat must be found.

Moral and religious questions aside, the option of active nonviolence deserves consideration on purely practical and political grounds. Political considerations can no longer justify the limitation of nonviolence to the area of one's individual life or that of small groups. Upon this political option, made ultimately on the level of national states, depends the life or death of the human species. Gandhi was the first, in the industrial era, to theorize, systematize, and apply in practice, in the political arena, methods of combat that do not aim at the death of the adversary and do not eliminate the possibility of reconciliation. In Brazil I have tried to contribute my own experiments to the development of this theory and practice.

Translated by Robert R. Barr.

In this chapter I am concerned with the dynamic of collective nonviolence in the face of collective violence. First of all, it is important to note that collective and individual violence are not the same thing. A blow is not a war.

To be sure, there are points of contact between collective and individual violence. A society that fails to train its members in channeling their aggression will be fertile soil for collective violence. Some societies and cultures are more violent than others — more attuned to the mimetisms of appropriation and antagonism.

However, there is no direct connection between the violence of the criminal and the violence of a soldier in a war — between individual and collective violence. True, both deal death. But the two species of violence spring from basically different causes and are governed by basically different rules. Individual violence may well be adequately dealt with by ordinary psychiatry. Correlatively, collective nonviolence — our principal interest in these pages — will be defined as the outcome of an application of the rules of collective psychology to the resolution of social conflict.

OBEDIENCE VS. SUBMISSION

One of the most fundamental causes of collective violence is not aggressivity, but blind submission to authority. There is a great difference between obedience and submissiveness. Obedience is the free act by which I accept community discipline, in order to render group life possible. Submissiveness is a self-renunciation, a self-abandonment vis-á-vis authority. Submissiveness is following orders without asking oneself whether these orders are factors of life or of death.

A most interesting experiment has demonstrated the extent to which blind submissiveness to authority can be an essential explanation for the human being's capacity for lethal destruction.

Stanley Milgram is a North American psychologist. In one of his experiments he assigned three persons to tasks in his laboratory: one to direct the experiment (the experimenter), a "student" who would agree to be the subject of the experiment, and a "monitor." The experiment was described to the "student" and the "monitor" as a study in the effect of punishment on the learning process—here, memorization. The "student" was to commit to memory various lists of words. Each time he made a mistake, the "monitor" would push a button and administer an electric shock. Would this punishment help or hinder the "student" in his efforts to learn? This was the announced purpose of the experiment.

Now the experimenter guided the "monitor" to an electric switchboard. Pushing any of the more than thirty buttons there would release an electric current, the experimenter explained, each at a different voltage. The first button discharged a 30-volt current, the next a higher voltage, and so on, all the way to the last button, which controlled a 450-volt current. The higher voltages, the experimenter explained, were dangerous, of course. And warning lights would indicate the degree of danger: "Slight Shock"—"Caution"—"Dangerous."

The "student" was led to another room, and bound to a kind of electric chair, where he would "receive the electric shocks." And the experiment was under way.

But a ruse was being employed. The actual subject of the experiment was not to be the "student" at all, but the "monitor" at the switchboard. The "student" was a professional actor, who would only feign receiving electric shocks. He would not actually receive any. The real purpose of the experiment was to see how far the "monitor" would be willing to go in blindly obeying the experimenter's orders. How much pain was one human being willing to inflict on another under orders from a third party? Would the "monitor" be willing to cause a fellow human being extreme physical pain—or only slight? Would the "monitor" even be willing to place that human being's life at risk as long as a third party "took the responsibility"? The "monitor," in each repetition of the experiment, had been selected from the community at large and had not the slightest idea that it was he or she, and not the "student," who would be the subject of the experiment.

The result was astonishing. No one invited to participate in the experiment refused. No "monitor" stopped short of 300 volts. Sixty percent "went all the way"—sent a life-threatening "450 volts" through the actor's convulsed body. Milgram worked with widely different subjects, from all social classes and from various countries (the United States, Italy, Germany, South Africa, Australia, and so on, the experiment being repeated in all of these countries). The "experimenters"—the real monitors of the experiment—in their reports on each repetition, unanimously testified to the severe emotional distress of the actual subject of the test in each instance. Each "monitor" believed that the suffering of the "student" was real. At 75 volts, the "subject" in the chair would utter a cry. At 150 volts he would beg to be released from the chair. The higher the voltage, the more he begged. At 285 volts the reaction was a scream of agony. The monitor was in a state of progressively mounting interior conflict. He or she would have liked to break off the experiment, lest the "subject" be caused any more pain. On the other hand, the "monitor" had agreed to take part in the experiment, and was acting under the orders of the experimenter, who was of course bathed in an aura of scientific authority (including the magical white coat of the specialist!). But each time the "monitor" hesitated to continue, the experimenter would give the order to proceed.

Finally, when the "monitor" thought he or she was on the point of sending the hapless "subject" a shock of 450 volts, the experimenter would sternly declare: "The experiment requires the monitor to continue." "Monitors" no longer knew what to do. Their hearts began to pound, and they began to perspire. Then the following curious phenomenon was observed. Little by little, in order to palliate the excruciating interior conflict, the "monitor" began to transfer his or her attention from the victim to the apparatus and to the experimenter, while uttering phrases like, "Very well, if you take all the responsibility." Slowly but surely, the vast majority of those tested began to act as the irresponsible agents of a system. They ceased to take an interest in the effects their acts had on the victims, and began to concern themselves exclusively with obeying—with satisfying their superior and "doing a good job." A double process had been set in motion: an affective disengagement from the victim, and an identification with authority.

It is this double process that constitutes one of the most powerful causes of collective violence.

Milgram made another impressive finding. We are too san-
guine where human behavior is concerned. Milgram asked stu-
dents who knew just what the experiment was intended to
accomplish, and knew of the ruse it would employ, the question:
How many subjects do you estimate will *not* be willing to go all
the way to the full voltage? The average answer: 85 percent. The
correct answer: only 40 percent.

We have a false idea of the behavior of the average person,
of John Doe, and a false idea of the causes of violence. Those
who offered to participate in Stanley Milgram's experiment and
administer the electric shocks were absolutely normal persons,
having no special aggressive tendencies. But caught up in a coer-
cive system — in a strong relationship of authority/subjection (not
an irresistible relationship, however, as one was not under threat
of grave reprisals if one chose to disobey) — the vast majority
preferred to submit to that authority, and ignore the imperatives
of their conscience. Perhaps this is the experiment's most important lesson: "Normal individuals, without the least hostility
toward their victims, simply in the course of fulfilling their duty,
can become agents of a process of abominable social destruction."[2] Obedience considerably alleviates the sense of guilt
aroused by the order to kill.

The Eichmann Case

The persecution suffered by Jews in World War II, and the
conduct of the Nazi official Adolf Eichmann, who was charged
with responsibility for the death of millions of Jews, amply con-
firms this thesis. Eichmann, according to Hannah Arendt, was
not the cold monster presented by official propaganda, but simply an "average" person.[3] He was disturbed that there would be
so much bloodshed. But his principal concern was with his ca-
reer, and he had a great desire to please his superiors. A half
dozen psychiatrists certified that he was a "normal" subject in
his relationship with his wife and children — indeed, an "ideal
husband and father"! Nor did he have any fanatical hatred for
Jews. Then why this monstrous incapacity to distinguish good
from evil, this colossal lack of ethics? The only possible answer
is the one suggested by Milgram: *generally speaking, the average*

person is unable to disobey the social system to which he or she belongs. Eichmann continually repeated during his trial that he was "only obeying orders." And he testified: "I never killed a Jew. For that matter, I never killed a gentile. I never killed anyone at all."

"He was a monster not as an individual, but as a cog in a monstrous machine."[4]

PASSIVITY VS. RESISTANCE

Collective violence is inexplicable without the submission, not only of a great part of the body social, but of the victims themselves. This is a difficult truth to accept. Hannah Arendt aroused violent indignation when she maintained that, in a way, the Jews participated in their own persecution during World War II. It would be absurd and scandalous to say such a thing, of course, if she had meant that the Jews were actually the authors of their own genocide. No, it was the Nazis who were responsible for the apocalyptic destruction of the Jewish people. It was they who thought it out, planned it, and executed it. However, the mere passivity of the Jews (and gentiles) involved does not suffice to explain the dimensions of the wholesale massacre.

To be sure, passivity was an enormous factor in facilitating the violence. For example, the Christian churches, with the admirable exception of a few individuals, failed to take a clear position of denunciation. A false conception of prudence, of the "lesser evil," inspired them to opt for a "diplomatic" silence rather than for a prophetic denunciation that might have shaken some moral sense into a public opinion being flattened by the steamroller of a totalitarian system organized to murder. The passivity of the Jewish authorities, as well as that of the mass of persecutors, is all but incomprehensible. But we must put ourselves in their place. They were faced with massive, seemingly uncontrollable, continuous violence. In this case, within the population, a sense of prostration and resignation arises that is very like that of the complicity of nonresistance.

Do we not have the same thing today? The airing of a film like "The Day After"—after an all-out nuclear war—with its paltry results in terms of overall consciousness, betrays the feeling of helplessness entertained by a great part of the inhabitants of a threatened country. Recently, in Philadelphia, sirens announced a nuclear alert. No one reacted. Nobody changed plans. Cars continued moving through the streets, schools stayed in session, everything proceeded normally. After all, nothing could be done. So why bother?

The pacifists of Europe and North America are much criticized for their alleged sense of cowardly capitulation, sneeringly referred to as the "spirit of Munich." In reality, however, are they not merely resisting the lethal submissiveness that I am denouncing? It is their critics, not they, who are submitting, who are capitulating to the system—the system of "violence under orders." The more perceptive element in the pacifist movement does not cultivate a cowardly sense of servile submission—accepting slavery to save one's skin. On the contrary, these pacifists insist that there is such a thing as nonviolent, even military, combativeness. They cite the example of Poland, which continues its resistance despite the presence of a far more powerful enemy both within and without Polish society. And they add: the only enslaved humanity that has any hope of liberation is one that does not submit. A dead humanity cannot live again.

Passivity, then, explains a great deal. But we must go further. We actually find the victims actively cooperating with their murderers, as if cooperation might somehow appease the executioner! All of us who have not yet overcome the fear of death have the capacity to succumb to this foolish and demeaning logic: a little sycophancy to salvage some little remnant of life.

In the case of the Nazi persecution of the Jews, the truth is that, frequently, Jewish authorities furnished the infamous lists of those who would die in the death camps.[5] In certain not altogether rare instances, the SS determined the number, ages, sex, profession, and national origin of the victims to be deported, and the Jewish Council of Theresienstadt executed the directive—always in terms of the "lesser of two evils."[6] By murdering a few, we are saving many. Eichmann explains further:

> We were in constant contact with Jewish leaders. Obviously we had to be prudent here. We gave no orders. No one said to Jewish leaders, "You must, you are ob-

liged . . ." and so on — for the simple reason that this would not have made the job any easier. If your lieutenant dislikes what he does, he does a poor job. . . . We did everything we could to make the business, you might say, interesting.[7]

Eichmann's unconscious cynicism is even more repulsive than if it had been voluntary maliciousness. We are dealing with the most blatant moral somnambulism.

The tragic truth is that if the Jewish people had been disorganized and leaderless, there would have been a great deal of disorder and misery — but surely fewer victims!

Psychiatrist Bruno Bettelheim, a Jew and a survivor of Dachau (1938) and Buchenwald (1939), writes:

The SS state would never have been able to function without the cooperation of its victims. More specifically, the SS would have been unable to control the deportation camps without the collaboration of numerous prisoners, generally nonvolunteers, at times reluctant — but often, and much more than one could wish, lending their willing, and even zealous, cooperation.

And this perceptive Jew, this victim of the Nazis, adds:

Upon careful consideration, and in retrospect, it appears altogether clear that only a complete refusal to collaborate on the part of the Jews would have offered any chance whatever of obliging Hitler to seek out another solution.[8]

Every available measure was taken to seek out, infiltrate, demoralize, and terrorize the Jewish people. Even humanitarian organizations were prostituted to this end. The latter, with the encouragement of Jewish leaders, took a census of the Jewish population — and made extermination easier. There was the case of the Warsaw Judenrat (Jewish Council), whose first president, Adam Czerniakow, committed suicide on July 23, 1942, when he realized that the council was a tool of the extermination machine.[9] The same thing seems to be happening in Guatemala

today: organizations whose overt purpose is to assist the deci-
mated, terror-stricken population, are in fact being used by the
death squads and espionage agencies for their own violent ends,
probably against the will of the leaders of these organizations.
Any element in popular organization can be a two-edged sword,
unless those in charge of these organizations throw up a solid
wall of (nonviolent) combativeness against the oppressor and
reject the ultimately counterproductive tactics of the "lesser
evil." At the same time, of course, these organizations must be
shrewd. They must know how to maneuver. And they must be
careful not to be provoked to counterproductive actions.

It would be interesting to turn to Brazilian history, and analyze, in terms of these concepts, the history of black slavery. To
be sure, African resistance in our country was beset with obstacles, probably even greater obstacles than those encountered by
the Jewish resistance in Nazi Germany. The blacks arrived in
Brazil exhausted, stupefied, after a hellish voyage on which many
of them had perished. They spoke different languages, for they
came from different nations. How could the oppressed organize,
when they were joined neither by language nor by custom, awash
in a materially and more technically advanced society (in terms
of weapons, and so on)? Still, the blacks did learn to speak
Portuguese and communicate with one another. Here once more
we see the degrading nature of the owner-slave relationship.
"The dominant ideas are the ideas of the dominant class," said
Marx. One of the terrible things about slavery is that the mind,
the soul, of the slave is infected. The subjugated seek to please
their executioners by thinking as they do. Their own values flee
to the most sacred recesses of the individual or collective soul
of the massacred race, the region of religion. Hence it is that
the Africans of Brazil continued to express their blackness
mostly in the disguised celebration of their traditional religions.
Religion is the human soul's last bastion of resistance.

It is also from a starting point in religion that an enslaved
nation can often rise again. When all is said and done, the case
of the Afro-Brazilian blacks is a good example of this basic
element in the dynamics of violent oppression: the disunion of
the oppressed, who often outnumbered the oppressor, is not
owing solely to a lack of organization and resources. No, the evil

runs deeper than this. In the last analysis, the disunion of the oppressed is a cancer generated by the *fear of death.* To salvage a last vestige of life, the oppressed allow the oppressor to penetrate their midst. A fear of death can lead all the way to betrayal.

But even short of outright betrayal, the policy of the lesser evil nearly always leads to a greater evil, as it destroys the will to resist, and allows the enemy to insinuate their ideas and their presence not only into the midst of the oppressed nation, but into the very soul of the combatants. The policy of the lesser evil is a policy of demoralization, of complicity with the lie, and it becomes the destruction of one's own sisters and brothers. As Martin Luther King, Jr., said, we must be meek of heart but strong of soul. We have to "know the score."

Chapter 6

Breaking Out of the Spiral of Violence

In light of what I have been attempting to explain in earlier chapters, perhaps we may now be able to discover some basic attitudes that can provide the basis for an escape from the deadly clutches of violence, attitudes that can defuse the conflict. Dom Helder Câmara never tires of speaking of the "spiral of violence." The institutional violence of unjust economic and political structures sooner or later generates an insurrectional violence on the part of the oppressed—which, in turn, sparks a greater violence on the part of the oppressor in the form of repression. How can we break out of this spiral?

RETURN TO THE OBJECT

The first such attitude, to resume Girard's analyses, will be to return to the object of the conflict. We must abandon a rivalry of persons and restrict ourselves to a conflict over the object alone. We must concentrate not on *who*, but *what*, is involved. As we have seen, mimetism tends to withdraw us from the struggle for the appropriation of an object, and suck us into the maelstrom of a personal antagonism.

One path by which we must return to the object is that of

Translated by Robert R. Barr.

careful investigation. We must expound, with great precision, the facts that have given rise to the struggle, in order to be able to speak on the basis of facts and not empty notions. Gandhi always began his campaigns with a minutely detailed presentation of his version of the facts, and he challenged his adversaries to do the same.

One of us who lives in a slum neighborhood recalls spending three months striving to bring the members of a mothers' club to accept mutual reconciliation—going from house to house to hear each member's version of the difficulties, completing and checking her testimony, then submitting each side's assessment of the facts to the scrutiny of the other side, and finally establishing a platform of mutual agreement on the *facts*. Without this laborious preliminary, it would have been impossible to bring all the mothers together for a meeting of reconciliation. Passion—the imitation of rivalry—would have prevented the reconstitution of the tissue of facts.

This experience makes it easy to see why it should be so irritating and harmful for persons of good will to saunter onto the scene with stereotyped phrases like "forgive and forget!," "bury the hatchet!," "Christians should love one another," and so on. Persons like these remind us of the friends of Job. When all is said and done, they have no genuine love for their suffering friends. They are so filled with their hypocritical "good conscience"—self-righteousness—that they easily spare themselves the inconvenience of getting involved in the conflict. "At least I didn't get into it. I've got self-control. I didn't get mixed up in that mess." We have a saying: "peace is the fruit of justice." And we have learned this from centuries of actual experience. As long as anyone must bear unjust blame in the place of others, the fire of discord will continue to smolder. Its live coals may flare up at any moment, and there will be a new conflagration.

A second way to return the object to the focus of the antagonists' attention is to *dramatize* the injustice committed with respect to the possession of the object of contention. In doing so, we shall reveal the identity of the innocent victim. This is what Solomon did in the case of the two women who had entered into competition over a newborn child, which each claimed was hers. When Solomon dramatized the affair, ordering the child to be cut in two to satisfy both "mothers," his artifice revealed the true mother: "Please, my lord, give her the living child — please do not kill it!" cried the one who had really borne the child, in her anxiety to save it. The other woman revealed her lie by saying, "It shall be neither mine nor yours. Divide it!" (1 Kings 3:26). With the disclosure of the lie, justice appeared, and peace returned. And we note that Solomon's dramatization caused public opinion to shift en bloc to the side of the innocent victim (1 Kings 3:28).

Active nonviolence always seeks to mediate the conflict by appealing to a third party — usually, public opinion, which will force the adversaries to emerge from their rivalry of pure competition and give an honest account of their respective claims to the disputed object. The conflict of personal rivalry is irrational, and frequently blind as well.

This is precisely the purpose, or one of the purposes, of the public fast. Through the voluntary suffering of those who have undertaken the fast, the problem is dramatized, and the hidden suffering of the victims of injustice is revealed. In the course of a fast in the public square on Christmas of 1983 to protest hunger and unemployment (in solidarity with fasts being conducted in 23 other cities), I wrote the following words: "By refusing to take nourishment, and by doing so publicly, we are 'dramatizing,' in the good sense of the word, the suffering of the millions who have no way to make their own cry heard."

The more prestigious the personage undertaking the fast, the more powerful the effect of the fast. This is how Gandhi managed to touch the conscience of so many millions — to paralyze conflicts in which frenzied multitudes already stood face to face. At the moment of the partition of India, he remained alone in Calcutta on a death fast. He succeeded in halting the slaughter between Muslims and Hindus. Which of the two communities wished to have Gandhi's death on its conscience? After all, this sufferer was obviously altogether innocent. It was the genius of Gandhi to reverse the data of the problem. "If you want to kill one another, my death will be the price you shall have to pay." It is psychologically impossible to slay a lamb of God (an innocent victim in free self-immolation) when the masses of the people are conscious of this victim's innocence.

Jesus died because the chief priests, the elders, the Pharisees, and the Herodians had successfully mounted a partial deception of the people as to his innocence. We know the vacillating attitude of the disciples on the road to Emmaus. Through his suffering, Gandhi dramatized the object of the conflict.

A third way of turning attention to the object of the conflict is to *symbolize* it. This is precisely what Gandhi did when, on April 6, 1930, in a symbolic gesture of ingenious simplicity, he gathered a handful of salt from the shore of the Indian Ocean. He thereby revealed to all Hindus that, in their own country, they had no civil right to undertake anything on their own initiative, not even the gathering of a little salt! And this in turn made it clear that English law in India, which had constituted the salt trade a monopoly of the colonial government, had actually monopolized the whole country. Through this act of conscientization Gandhi conveyed to the entire nation of India his implicit invitation to massive disobedience wherever the English colonial institution was concerned, and to a march toward the independence of the nation. Salt would be the symbolic representation of the oppressed homeland, a land to be liberated. It "visualized," rendered visible, the object of the conflict.

Ultimately, active nonviolence always tries to do three things:

1. Turn the attention of the antagonists to the object of contention.

2. Appeal to a third party, usually the public at large, to pressure the rivals to desist from a confrontation that has taken the form of personal rivalry. Get them to return to an "objective" rivalry. In other words, mediate the conflict.

3. This does not mean striking a compromise. On the contrary, the third thing active nonviolence tries to do is find a powerful symbol, capable of:

a. Moving the hearts and minds of the people, so that the masses will cease to be mere spectators; so that they will mobilize and join the conflict.

b. Showing forth the shining innocence of the righteous victim (or cause), and thus short-circuiting the constant attempt to reestablish a false social peace by victimizing a scapegoat.

c. Revealing what is really at stake in the conflict. What is the object of contention? To the eyes of the uninformed, the object nearly always disappears behind the smokescreen of incomprehensible discourse and involuted disputes.

RELATE TO THE ADVERSARY

In order to break out of the spiral of collective violence, it will not suffice to turn the attention of the competitors and participants to the object of contention. One must also know how to relate to one's adversary. In a case of violent collective conflict, both the oppressed and the oppressor invariably disguise the face of their respective enemies. They dub their adversary beasts, animals, pigs, butchers, and so forth. But the disguise is counterproductive. It incriminates the adversary, but it also unites them. The employee tends to see all employers in the same image, with individual differences and personal characteristics simply disappearing. And employers conceptually reduce their employees to such-and-such an amount of replaceable "manpower."

But this sort of psychological oversimplification is devastating for a resolution of conflict, especially for the victim, for it cements over many "chinks" through which one's relationship with the adversary might otherwise have been modified. If all the soldiers who expel slum-dwellers from their shacks are no more than equal pieces in a repressive machine, if all members of a death squad are looked upon as identical, and identically beastly, by their victims, the victims, willy-nilly, are simply reinforcing their oppressors' internal unity. We must be able to appraise our relationship with our adversary with neither arrogance nor servility.

Three attitudes psychologically dehumanize the adversary and thereby aggravate conflict. They are fear, murder, and contempt. Contempt is tantamount to moral murder. To despise someone is to tell him or her, mentally, "As far as I'm concerned, you're dead." In the typical instance, the moral murderer will be the oppressor. But the courageous oppressed are capable of contemptuous attitudes and behavior, as well. (The cowardly oppressed restrict their attitudes to those of fear and hatred.)

Here too, in as unequal and violent a struggle as that between oppressed and oppressor, the oppressed must turn their attention to the object sought. (The object may actually belong to the oppressed in virtue of the very laws of the oppressor!) Then, fearlessly, but without arrogance, in regard for each member of the oppressing group as an individual with a particular psychology different from that of another member, the oppressed must find a way to enter into contact with this individual and make of him or her a demand that is actually within his or her power to grant.

I recall a slum-razing in which the soldiers were treated by their victims as human beings, and politely, but without servility, requested to comply with the law requiring an inventory of the contents of each shack before the expulsion of the family. But this is practically impossible, unless the expulsion is to drag on forever. The respect accorded them by the inhabitants of the slum moved the soldiers to take their request seriously, and the neighborhood was spared destruction for the moment. There have been innumerable cases, and far more drastic ones, along the same lines, in Guatemala, in El Salvador, and, in bygone days, in the Nazi death camps. Even in these situations, the psychology of the relationship between executioners and victims has been most interesting.

We must never forget that the mechanisms of collective violence function on the basis of submission to orders on the part of the executioner. Not rarely, observant victims make use of the very regulations laid down by the oppressor, or the words of the order, to disorient the activity of the executioners, or to obtain advantages that other victims, terror-stricken or rebellious, have failed to win. We must study our enemies' mental system most carefully, especially if they are particularly monstrous in their attitudes and behavior, and thereby discover the chinks in their armor through which they may be approachable or even vulnerable. We must always resist the temptation to reduce each individual oppressor to a carbon copy of a single original.

Finally, there are Lanza del Vasto's five possible ways of relating to a conflict, as follows.

Neutrality

So-called neutrality is actually a way of striking a relationship to a conflict. I "don't get involved." It is a relationship bereft of commitment, then. But it is a relationship, because, for example, I exercise a function that involves having to judge between the parties in confrontation. I am a father, a mother, a bishop, a judge, a priest, a friend of both parties, or the like, and I find persons somehow dependent upon me to be in a state of struggle.

The case of Pilate is typical. Pilate was not directly interested in a conflict among Jews. Nevertheless, his function obliged him to take a position. He selected that of neutrality. But neutrality is never really neutral. It ultimately decides against the weaker party. Pilate's neutrality condemned Jesus. Pilate finally "washed his hands of the matter," and Jesus the Righteous One was eliminated.

Omission

To "relate" to a conflict by omission is to fail to maintain any relationship whatever with the conflict, whether in virtue of my function or by reason of anything else. For example, I see a street fight, or am present at an attempted murder, and I refuse to "get involved." I turn my back. I run away.

Capitulation

Another way of "confronting" conflict is by capitulation. I implore, I beg for mercy. I cry out, "Please don't murder me!" Ultimately it is fear of death or injury that governs my behavior, not love of justice. I introject, I interiorize, a servile attitude, the attitude of a slave. I am drawn into the lethal dialectic of owner and slave, oppressor and oppressed.

Violent Struggle

If I engage in violent struggle, at least I am not a coward. I take sides. I try to discern which of the opposing causes is the just cause, and I struggle to defend the interests of that side. But I have allowed the aggressor to choose the weapons. I take an eye for an eye, a tooth for a tooth. I return violence for violence. At least this attitude is superior to the previous three. As Gandhi said: If you cannot be nonviolent, at least be violent. But do *something*.

Active Nonviolence

The fifth way of confronting a struggle is by active nonviolence. Active nonviolence is no wonder drug. It does not achieve its effect quickly. It must be persevering. It involves the gospel paradox:

> When a person strikes you on the right cheek, turn and offer him the other. If anyone wants to go to law over your shirt, hand him your coat as well. Should anyone press you into service for one mile, go with him two miles [Matt. 5:39–41].

Note well: by doing so, you are not neutral, you are not remiss, you do not flee, or retreat, or capitulate. You remain firm, and refuse to release your adversary until the conflict is resolved. You offer what you are and what you have—your coat, your whole body—until you and your adversary reach a solution.

Arraigned before Pilate, Jesus practiced the fifth way:

> One of the guards who was standing nearby gave Jesus a sharp blow on the face. "Is that the way to answer the high priest?" he said. Jesus replied, "If I have said anything wrong, produce the evidence; but if I spoke the truth, why hit me?" [John 18:22-23].

Jesus offered not just "the other cheek," but his entire body. He did not flinch. He did not recoil. He did not capitulate. He practiced nonviolence, with constancy and pertinacity. With a question—neither an arrogant one nor a subservient one—he called for objectivity. And his point of departure was in an objective fact: a blow to the face.

CIVIL DISOBEDIENCE

An attitude of active nonviolence will fail to offer an effective remedy for violence unless it is provided with a third element. It will not be enough to return to the object of contention. Nor will it suffice to be able to relate to our adversary. It happens that, as our analyses have shown, the sine qua non of collective violence is neither hatred, nor perversity, but simply the submissiveness of a population to the orders of a minority. When all is said and done, it is the convenient, comfortable thoughtlessness (cowardice?) of "honest citizens," who constitute the majority of the population, that is the great culprit where collective violence is concerned.

First, we must *train the masses in civil disobedience* — along the lines of active nonviolence, with profound respect for the life and love for the person who is our adversary. This will not be a matter of casual improvisation. It will mean an arduous struggle — a spiritual struggle as much as a political one. Saint Paul speaks of shameful silence. The people of God must learn *not* to keep silent, to disobey, when sin threatens to prevail in society. Law is made for human beings, not human beings for law. How long do we intend to tolerate the death by starvation of millions of our own sisters and brothers?

In the second place, *the power of nonviolence is in the number of persons it can reach.* The methods of active nonviolence can be practiced by anyone. They are not the monopoly of trained guerrillas. The huge number of our poor, and the strategic place they occupy in the economy (as it is they who wield the mattocks and drive the machinery) will have their effect only if we emerge from our local struggles. What is the tragedy of Central America? Perhaps, very simply, the fact that popular struggles erupt only locally, to be combated by a much larger, multinational, force of repression.

The nonviolent struggle must not be a matter of improvisation, then. It cannot be skylifted to the battleground by helicopter. When an entire historical process is obviously headed for a violent denouement, we shall not suddenly be able to improvise an alternative. Meanwhile, wherever the popular struggle is unable to make the most of the advantages we have indicated above—wherever it continues to be merely local, so that it will be without massive popular support—it will inevitably be either crushed, absorbed by nonrevolutionary elements, or forced to take up arms lest it see its more active members, if not indeed entire peoples, barbarously annihilated. In the second place, then, it is our duty to render the nonviolent struggle a viable alternative by creating a continental network for a popular struggle that will thus enjoy international support.

SHAKING OFF THE FEAR OF DEATH

There is another condition for vanquishing collective violence. What is the basic, rock-bottom element in the passivity of the masses who so unprotestingly submit to the injustice being done them? Fear of losing their lives. Our surrender of our lives to God is obviously not what it ought to be, then. Thus the basic challenge facing us today is to find a way to win the adherence of the people by showing them that our methods of struggle are ultimately more effective and less dangerous than either a passivity of accommodation or an armed revolution. The purity of our means, the intelligent selection of symbolic actions calculated to move the noblest part of the popular conscience, the careful construction of a network of ever broader and broader struggle (campaigns of disobedience), and the clarity of the political objectives we seek, are the four essential conditions for the credibility of the nonviolent alternative in the coming years. And we must act very quickly. There is little time left. Evidently we shall have to achieve our goal through an elite corps of popular leaders deeply bound to their communities, and trained and disciplined in a very practical way, but unafraid of the theory that can shed light on this practicality of theirs.

There is still a great deal of intellectual and organizational prejudice among us. Frequently we rely on talent and "having a knack" for what needs to be done rather than on hard work. Do capitalists, even Brazilian capitalists, rely on their "knack" in doing business and repressing the people? No, here everything is very carefully planned out in advance. Our nonviolence seems still a chaotic, disorganized project, lacking ideological solidity and spiritual purity. We have no competent instructors. Furthermore, we have faith without works. We must work harder and be more pure.

LOVE OF ENEMY

The ultimate condition for breaking out of the circle of violence, then, will be a love for our enemy. This means that we have enemies—even class enemies. But nonviolence will be shrewd enough to discover the chinks in their armor, through which it can reach the human part within them, and thus dismantle their system of defenses. Humility, then—the acknowledgment of our own errors—will be a basic part of our strategy.

Chapter 7

The Meaning of Fasting

FOUR APPROACHES TO FASTING

Physical. When correctly carried out, a fast can contribute a great deal to our physical health. It gives our bodily organs, like the stomach and the liver, some "time off." It purifies the system.

As a flower can live for a long period of time in a vase of water, so the human body, which is 90 percent water, can maintain its basic activities for more than forty days on an intake of water alone.

Psychological. Fasting can play a *psychological* role. A public refusal to take nourishment dramatizes the plight of the suffering millions who cannot make their cry heard. No one listens to the poor, the Bible says (Prov. 21:13). When a group of persons, or better, a person *respected and loved* by the community, undertakes a fast, the suffering of the little ones of the earth comes at last to public attention. Far from attracting attention to themselves, the fasters become *symbolic persons*, calling public attention to a reality far more tragic than the one they behold (the fast). They call public attention to the silent suffering of millions of persons who cannot themselves persuade anyone to listen to them. Recently we participated in a Christmas fast in order to

Translated by Robert R. Barr.

attract the attention of the public to the "silent war of hunger" that is killing more persons than the war between Iran and Iraq.

We tell persons whose compassion we have aroused: Do you feel sorry for us because we go for a week or ten days without eating? You would do better to look at the far more terrible suffering of persons who "fast" all year round—who are hungry to the point of malnutrition!

To borrow an image from the world of sports: now the ball is in their court. Now what are the persons whose attention we have turned to the plight of the poor going to do? The suffering of the little, the lowly, escapes the pain of the individual conscience, for the misery of the lowly "slips through the cracks" of society and is lost—lost under the bridges, on the sidewalks, in prison, in the slums, in the factories. No one cares about the dregs of humanity.

Even a slum is *physically* small. Swallowed up in the big city, the shacks look like doll houses. Wealthy tourists passing through do not even notice them. One of the psychological purposes of fasting, in keeping with the principles of mass psychology, is to shift all this suffering into the public gaze through the use of a symbol, so that this misery may reach the conscience of millions, and thereby paralyze the conflicts of frenzied multitudes in confrontation.

If I fast, this will produce a certain effect. But if the local bishop fasts, especially if he is someone bound to the people by ties of friendship and respect, the effect will be far more powerful. Let us note: a fast is not a hunger strike. In a hunger strike you try to pressure your enemy, the oppressor. In a fast, you address the conscience of your *friends*. You fast "against" your friends, not your enemies. You say: "You who trust me and love me—don't just stand there! Come join me in the fight against hunger!"

Religious. Before all else, fasting is a *religious* act. As a religious act, it is first and foremost an act of humility. The person fasting acknowledges before God and humanity alike his or her emptiness of God. "I am hungry for food, yes. But I am far more hungry for the divine presence. I seek purification, in the hope that God will dwell in me once more. Come live with us, God-with-us, Emmanuel!"

Political. Finally, fasting has a *political* purpose. It sensitizes the masses. It reaches the conscience of comfortable friends. It touches the noblest nerves of the multitude. And before you know it, it arouses a colossal popular energy. And that energy begins to change the course of history, simply through dialogue, noncooperation, and civil disobedience (general strikes and boycotts). All of this transpires under the inspiration of a spirituality of active nonviolence. Better to die than to kill, you cry! Yes, you respect your enemy this much. And suddenly the old objection is irrelevant; but the poor go hungry all year long! Why ask them to shoulder the additional burden of a voluntary fast? Once when this question was asked in a San Salvador slum, one of the persons who lived in the slum responded: "Oh, is fasting, too, something only the rich have a right to?"

PUBLIC FASTING: THE BIBLICAL BASIS

The Bible mentions public fasting very often:

Jehosaphat was frightened, and he hastened to consult the Lord. He proclaimed a fast for all Judah [2 Chron. 20:3].

Then I proclaimed a fast, there by the river of Ahava, that we might humble ourselves before our God to petition from him a safe journey [Ezra 8:21].

On the twenty-fourth day of this month, the Israelites gathered together fasting and in sackcloth, their heads covered with dust [Neh. 9:1].

In the ninth month, in the fifth year of Jehoiakim ... a fast to placate the Lord was proclaimed for all the people of Jerusalem and all who came from Judah's cities to Jerusalem [Jer. 36:9].

Consider especially this text from the prophet Joel, showing what an important part fasting played among the customs of God's people in time of great need:

Gird yourselves and weep, O priests!
          wail, O ministers of the altar!
Come, spend the night in sackcloth,
          O ministers of my God!
The house of your God is deprived
          of offering and libation.
Proclaim a fast,
          call an assembly;
Gather the elders,
          all who dwell in the land,
Into the house of the Lord, your God,
          and cry to the Lord!
                    [Joel 1:13-14].

In the biblical tradition, it is not the material element in fasting that constitutes a deed of authentic repentance. The prophetical tradition of Israel places a great deal of insistence on the possible deviations here. For example, let us recall the celebrated text of the prophet Isaiah that places in God's mouth the following words:

Tell my people their wickedness,
          and the house of Jacob their sins.
They seek me day after day,
          and desire to know my ways. . . .
They ask me . . .
"Why do we fast, and you do not see it?
          Afflict ourselves, and you take no note of it?"
Lo, on your fast day you carry out your own pursuits,
          and drive all your laborers.
Yes, your fast ends in quarreling and fighting,
          striking with wicked claw.
Would that today you might fast
          so as to make your voice heard on high!
Is this the manner of fasting I wish,
          of keeping a day of penance:
That a man bow his head like a reed,
          and lie in sackcloth and ashes?
Do you call this a fast,

a day acceptable to the Lord?
This, rather, is the fasting that I wish:
     releasing those bound unjustly,
     untying the thongs of the yoke;
Setting free the oppressed,
     breaking every yoke;
Sharing your bread with the hungry,
     sheltering the homeless;
Clothing the naked when you see them,
     and not turning your back on your own.
Then your light shall break forth like the dawn,
     and your wound shall quickly be healed. . . .
Then you shall call, and the Lord will answer,
     you shall cry for help, and he will say: Here I am!
                                 [Isa. 58:1-9].

And so on, all through chapter 58.

Zachariah 7:5, 9-10 makes the same point. Authentic fasting must be an act leading to charity and justice toward one's neighbor, toward the poor and the lost.

Jesus completes this prophetical teaching, alerting us to the danger of hypocrisy that lurks in fasting or any other religious act that can win us the undeserved reputation of being righteous men and women. We hear Jesus' warning at the beginning of the sixth chapter of Saint Matthew. It applies to any religious activity, whether it be fasting, prayer, or helping one's neighbor:

Be on guard against performing religious acts for people to see. Otherwise expect no recompense from your heavenly Father [Matt. 6:1].

More specifically with regard to fasting, Jesus says:

When you fast, you are not to look glum as the hypocrites do. They change the appearance of their faces so that others may see they are fasting. I assure you, they are already repaid. . . . No one can see you are fasting but your Father who is hidden; and your Father who sees what is hidden will repay you [Matt. 6:13–14].

In conclusion, let us note that the purpose of any activity of conversion is *charity*. Fasting is valid as a gesture of humility. The sinner, or, collectively, a sinful people, acknowledge that a clean break must be made with unjust, sinful activities, and that without the coming of a Savior they will lack the strength to lift themselves out of the pit of evil into which they have fallen. The reason they fast is to have the strength to practice right and justice vis-à-vis their sisters and brothers. They run the serious risk of attracting attention to themselves with this courageous penitential attitude of theirs, and thus of falling into a kind of vanity and self-satisfaction. This sense of empty contentment will then be the sole reward that these self-styled repentant sinners will receive.

These dangers, however, do not invalidate a collective act of prayer and fasting. Public deeds of this nature can wake persons up, can grasp persons of good will by the lapels and shake them, so that they turn away, they and their nations, from the evil they are committing. This is what the citizens of Nineveh did upon hearing the preaching of the prophet Jonah:

> Jonah. . . . had gone but a single day's walk announcing, "forty days more and Nineveh shall be destroyed," when the people of Nineveh believed God; they proclaimed a fast and all of them, great and small, put on sackcloth. . . . When God saw by their actions how they turned from their evil way, he repented of the evil that he had threatened to do to them; he did not carry it out [Jonah 3:4-5, 10].

Chapter 8

Class Struggle and the Gospel

JESUS AND CLASS STRUGGLE

Class struggle is not the only mover of history. There are phases in history when the current that sweeps persons up and gets them moving does not issue principally from class struggle. There were the wars of religion, for example, or the patriotic wars.

It is erroneous, then, to absolutize class struggle as if it were the only motive force in history. But it would be equally absurd to deny the class struggle the role it does play in social progress. The history of industrial societies, these last hundred years, is ongoing evidence of this role. It was by the class struggle that these societies, in many places, were improved, that injustice retreated, and that the condition of the working classes ceased to be what it had been. Without the class struggle, would there be free unions today?

The question is whether this crucial historical element, class struggle, must be a stranger to charity.

Jesus' celebrated injunction, "Love your enemies" (Luke 6:27), means, first of all, that we have enemies. And in order to

Translated by Robert R. Barr.

turn the other cheek, one must select an active attitude of confrontation with someone who is unjust. Cowardice will never receive a slap in the face, because cowardice will never confront the enemy "face to face," as a human being. It will be dead, and will usually seize upon the "solution" of fleeing or hiding. Jesus, in the clutches of the chief priests in Jerusalem, upon receiving a blow in the face, offered the perfect example of active evangelical resistance: he openly denounced the evil, without using the weapons of the oppressor (lying and violence). He pinned the unjust aggressor to the wall with a question sharp as a dagger: "I have spoken publicly to anyone who would listen. . . . There was nothing secret about anything I said." Jesus' attitude was basically open and public, although he did keep certain strategies secret during his public life because the "hour" of the definitive conflict had not yet arrived. "Why do you question me? . . . If I said anything wrong, produce the evidence; but if I spoke the truth, why hit me?" (John 18:20–23).

There can be no doubt about it. The gospel proposes a most original manner of waging a conflict, although it is one with roots in the Old Testament. Hence Jesus' famous words, so familiar to us all:

> To you who hear me, I say: Love your enemies, do good
> to those who hate you; bless those who curse you and pray
> for those who maltreat you. When someone slaps you on
> one cheek, turn and give him the other; when someone
> takes your coat, let him have your shirt as well [Matt. 6:27–
> 29].

"If you love those who love you, what credit is that to you?" (Luke 6:32). Capitalists do that! To possess the land—to have a decisive influence on history and on other persons—according to Jesus, one must be lowly. "Blest are the lowly; they shall inherit the land" (Matt. 5:5). Yes, lowly; but energetic! For example, when the lowly Jesus expels the buyers and sellers from the temple, or when he calls the Pharisees a brood of vipers, Herod a fox, and Peter Satan—here is a lowly one with a great deal of energy! But he eventually overcomes the temptation to violence, if indeed he has ever really suffered it. He had sent his disciples out preaching in Galilee without purse or staff. But in Luke 22:35–36 they must suddenly take not only a purse, but a sword as well, even if they must sell their clothes in order to buy them! The disciples respond, "Lord, here are two swords!" And Jesus answers: "Enough." But in the prison scene, Jesus tells the disciple who had taken up the sword: "Enough!" (Luke 22:51); and in Matthew 26:52 he adds: "Those who use the sword are sooner or later destroyed by it."

How are we to explain this seemingly paradoxical attitude, at once violent and peace-loving, on Jesus' part?

We have only to notice: *the "violence of the gospel" never employs the weapons of death and contempt,* the two great arms of the violent of all times. The contempt of the violent consists in "writing off" a person as no longer existing. "As far as I'm concerned, you're already dead," the violent seem to say. The physical death of one's enemies is the radical way not to have enemies. Physical death and moral death (vilification) are the twin objectives sought by "normal" combatants when they run out of other solutions. Christ refused to avail himself of this means. He had hard words for his enemies, yes. But he never scorned them. For him they were always "persons." Fanaticism consists in preferring ideas to friendship. Christ was never a fanatic, then, for he never sacrificed human beings to his ideas. He sacrificed only himself, for the sake of the reign of God. And he invited his disciples to do the same, so long as they did it freely.

For Jesus, the person most suitable to receive his message continues to be the one invited to his wedding banquet. Like his Father, he makes the sun of his love to shine on good and evil persons indiscriminately. If we would see the weeds separated from the wheat, we must await the time of harvest.

Another observation will aid us in our comprehension. It concerns the *socio-political situation* in which Jesus found himself — the political, historical situation he had to face "at that time," in that part of the Roman empire to which his land of Palestine belonged. The Roman empire was at the height of its power. Any armed revolt mounted against that empire would inevitably end in catastrophe. The Roman forces of repression were incomparably more powerful than any army of liberation or groups of guerrillas. Nevertheless, in Jesus' land and time, certain armed organizations were preparing for a struggle with the dominant classes and with Roman imperialism. They were called Zealots.

Jesus was definitely in contact with Zealot groups, and his preaching and activity had various points in common with them. He called the people to freedom, and to a society of sharing and justice. He defended the poor. He fearlessly attacked the rich, the high priests, the lawyers, and the Pharisees—that is, the lords of wealth, the political authorities, and the professors of the dominant ideology. His prestige with the crowds was enormous, and the Zealots repeatedly sought to take advantage of his extraordinary influence over the masses to make him the leader of a national revolution. After the multiplication of the loaves, enthusiastics, perhaps encouraged by the Zealots, wished to make their king:

> When the people saw the sign he had performed they began to say, "This is undoubtedly the Prophet who is to come into the world." At that, Jesus realized that they would come and carry him off to make him king, so he fled back to the mountain alone [John 6:14–15].

The apostles themselves were not immune to temptations arising from Jesus' political prestige. For that matter, a number of them had probably come from the ranks of the Zealots—Simon Peter, for example, or Judas, the betrayer, whose nickname—"Iscariot" or *Sicarius*—meant the wielder of a *sica* or dagger. After all, in Jesus' time as in our own, guerrillas did not go about unarmed. They were usually poor country folk, refugees from the great farming tracts where they had been exploited by the local aristocracy. They hid in the wasteland, and swooped down like wolves to perpetrate their assaults on government convoys or travelers' caravans. They were ultra-nationalistic, anti-Roman, anti-high priest, poor, and ready to sacrifice their lives for the liberation of their country. Their courage and their destitution fit them right in with the rest of Jesus' group. They no more had a stone on which to lay their head than did their master.

If, as is probable, there were two declared Zealots among the twelve apostles, it is understandable that the other ten would have been sympathetic to their cause. James and John, the sons of Zebedee, or "sons of thunder," as Jesus called them because of their fiery temperament, wanted to be the prime ministers of Jesus' kingdom, which they conceptualized as a military regime. One day they sent their mother to ask Jesus to install them "one at your right and the other at your left" (Mark 10:37) after he should take power.

Peter, the leader of the twelve, shared this popular nationalistic ideology to the point that one day he sought to turn Jesus aside from his mission. And when Judas betrayed him, perhaps it was in deep embitterment at Jesus' refusal to use his extraordinary influence with the people in order to assume power. Judas may have wished to oblige Jesus to make use of this power by "setting him up"—by having him arrested in the Garden of Olives. There, when the Master so unexpectedly continued to refuse to resist, Judas, in despair at the certain death his friend now faced, "went off and hanged himself" (Matt.27:5).

On various occasions the crowds clearly manifested their desire to mount an armed nationalistic revolution, expel the Romans, and proclaim their national leader king of the Jews. So evident was their intention that their motto was inscribed over Jesus' head as he hung on the cross. "Jesus of Nazareth, King of the Jews" is an expression of the principal reason for his death sentence at the hands of the Romans. Pontius Pilate, the Roman official who presided at Jesus' trial, knew perfectly well that Jesus had no wish to be king. "I find no case against this man" (John 18:38), he declared, and sought to acquit him. But the crowd preferred to rescue Barabbas, probably a guerrilla captured in the course of an attempted Zealot coup. Fernando Belo writes:

> Apparently the crowd did an about-face. We have always seen them supporting Jesus in the scenes in the vicinity of the temple. These were the petite bourgeoisie of Jerusalem, economically dependent on the temple. Naturally they supported Jesus when he seized the temple to do battle with the classes that oppressed them, just as they

would resist the Zealots in 66–77. But once it became clear
that Jesus' aims were not those of the Zealots, and especially not those of the temple, it was logical, in a materi-
alistic logic, that the crowd would follow their class
interests and call for the liberation of a Zealot who had
been a hero of the resistance: Barabbas.[1]

And so we have a reconciliation of the two political extremes.
The conservatives and reactionaries of the dominant class (the
high priests, the members of Herod's party, and the Sadducees)
connive with the national liberation movement (the Zealots and
Pharisees) to do away with Jesus. Jesus had become a threat to
both tendencies. In the mind of the conservatives, the high
priests and other Sadducees, Jesus might easily provoke Roman
repression:

> "What are we to do," they said, "with this man performing
> all sorts of signs? If we let him go on like this, the whole
> world will believe in him. Then the Romans will come in
> and sweep away our sanctuary and our nation" [John
> 11:47–48].

For the ultra-nationalists, Jesus was a danger because he side-
tracked the people. He turned them aside from an armed struggle, and had other objectives besides national liberation. He
threw the whole struggle out of kilter.

JESUS AND ARMED STRUGGLE

And so the question arises, altogether naturally: Why does
Jesus renounce armed struggle? It seems to me that there are
two main reasons.

Jesus is a penetrating observer of the political reality of his
time. He clearly perceives that *the balance of power does not favor
the success of an armed revolution.* As we have observed, the
Roman empire was at the height of its power. Anyone attacking
the class installed in power by the Roman empire—anyone attacking Herod and the high priests—would inevitably be crushed
to powder. This analysis is abundantly confirmed by the events

of the Jewish war of A.D.70. Nearly forty years after Jesus' death, the Zealots did mount their long desired popular uprising. The war lasted four bloody years, until the Roman general Titus finally quelled the revolt in a bloodbath, destroyed Jerusalem, and failed to prevent the burning of Herod's magnificent temple, whose destruction Jesus had prophesied. In conditions of weakness, a strategy of nonviolent, active resistance is more effective than armed revolt. What the gospel offers us here, in Jesus' practice and words, is a policy based on shrewd political wisdom.

But it is not for this reason alone that Jesus refuses to take up arms. The teacher from Nazareth is resisting an attitude that pervades the Zealot current, the soul of the whole people of Israel, and the disciples themselves. All of them are blindly nationalistic. The message of Christ goes much further. Jesus is far more radically revolutionary. His revolution embraces not only the Jerusalem temple and the land of Israel, but all men and women, including the gentiles. To take sides with the Zealots would have been to limit his message to the Jewish people, and launch a mere *reform* of the religion of Israel—a reform internal to the nation, rather than an international religious *revolution*.

But there is still more. Any partisan revolt—any revolt that includes only one nation or class of persons—no matter how valid it is in itself—is inevitably led to reconstitute a structure of domination. Being partisan, it must eliminate the other party in order to take power. If the main objective of the revolt is to *take power,* the group conducting the revolt will need pressure groups, base groups, and so on, culminating in a popular army, to *dominate* the adversary.

History proceeds from conflict to conflict, in dynamic tension. One must create an "antagonistic" force—one that "struggles against." But this is just the problem. How can conflicts, antagonisms, be overcome, how can a final synthesis be reached in the form of a classless society without domination, *if the struggle itself utilizes the very arms of the dominant class? At the heart of evangelical nonviolence is this fundamental requirement: that the struggle be waged without using the arms of the oppressor, in order to achieve a genuinely new social situation. Use the weapons of the capitalist to overthrow capitalism and you are contaminated with capitalism.* To put it another way: Jesus warns, "those who use the sword are sooner or later destroyed by it" (Matt. 26:52). This logion contains a "political" truth: if, in struggling with an oppressor, I am creating a revolutionary counterpower, after the revolution mechanisms of domination will persist, which, precisely, I have sought to destroy. And these mechanisms will turn on me and destroy me.

I must be faithful to the dialectic to the very end. Combat, yes; but only a combat that introduces its "antagonism," its contradiction, into the very heart of praxis itself—that is, into the very manner of the struggle. If my enemy employs violence, I, in order to bring that enemy down, must use active nonviolence. It seems to me that Jesus, altogether aware of the political challenges of his time, sought on repeated occasions to convey the conviction that I have just expressed. His railings against kings (Herod) and the powerful are always vehement, and in this he is being faithful to a very ancient tradition of his people. As we read in the Book of Samuel, in a most radical condemnation of the actually prevailing system, the heads of the monarchical regime always end up taking the sons of the farmworkers for the king's army, their daughters for the king's bed, and their vineyards and plantations as fiefs of the crown.

Let us also recall the following wonderful condemnation of the mechanisms of power wheresoever they may be found. One day the disciples were disputing among themselves who would be the greatest in the reign of God to come. Jesus told them:

> Earthly kings lord it over their people. Those who exercise authority over them are called their benefactors. Yet it cannot be that way with you. Let the greater among you be as the junior, the leader as the servant. . . . I am in your midst as the one who serves you [Luke 22:25–27].

Fernando Belo, while not agreeing with the principle of nonviolence as we profess it, nevertheless states, most perceptively:

> The most difficult question is: the adoption of the same kind of methods of struggle as are used by the dominant class (for example, the use of mercenaries against the dom-

inant class) will be very likely, once victory is achieved, to become a dominating violence in its own turn, albeit that of another class. It is not indifferent, then, in a revolutionary struggle, which means are chosen to achieve the long-term goal, the elimination of the mechanisms of power of one class over another. The best way to struggle for power will be the one that permits the launching of a process that moves toward the elimination of the apparatus of state.[2]

And he concludes:

The power of a class that dominates through force of arms is a symptom of the bodily weakness of the elements of this class. Those who use weapons are weak without them.[3]

It seems to me that the proletariat, although objectively the stronger (at least potentially—in virtue of their numbers and the place they occupy in the economy), nevertheless should not take up arms, and ought to train themselves in a nonviolent strategy instead. By doing so they will create a genuinely new society—a society that will be a genuine community and hence a society that will transcend all dominations.

There are two different tendencies in the Marxist tradition. One, which we might call the Leninist tendency, aims first at seizing the power of state, and then at transforming structures. In other words it works from the top down. The Brazilian left, in thrusting this tendency to its extreme, has frequently fallen into two grave errors: elitism and vanguardism. How many are the tiny little organizations that regard themselves as so "enlightened" as to be the real truth of the proletariat, but that spend all their time ferreting out militants, without ever bothering to do any work at the grass roots, any real spadework!

The other tendency is more democratic. It works from the bottom up. It has more respect for work at the grass roots. Its goal is to effect a class liberation in certain sectors wherever possible, even though it may promise to be only a partial, temporary liberation. It begins by liberating such and such a base community, such and such a group in a factory, such and such a union zone, and so on—little experiments in socialization here and there, now and then, training the people by means of these "trial runs" and progressively extending these zones of liberation.

Surely it is clear that, politically, the gospel is on this second, non-Leninist side of the Marxist tradition. If liberation were one day to proceed in evangelical fashion, this is how it would proceed. For it is in this fashion that the mechanisms of power created by a popular force for liberation will be less totalitarian tomorrow.

PART TWO

NONVIOLENCE AND THE GOSPEL

Chapter 9

Grace and Power

A FRATERNAL QUESTION

This chapter was written at the time of the popular uprising in Nicaragua. It is the result of reflections made at that time by the Serviço Nacional Justiça e Não-Violência in Brazil in respect to events in Nicaragua and Central America. It was impossible for us not to take a positon.

Nicaragua in point of fact is a beacon of hope for all of Latin America. And its Christians participated and still participate en masse in the popular uprising, as they do also in El Salvador. Among them were a number of priests, in particular two, Miguel d'Escoto and Ernesto Cardenal, who had begun their revolutionary pilgrimage by advocating active nonviolence. Miguel, in an important article, "The Power of the Cross" (published in the *Catholic Worker* in 1979 and based on an interview of December 1978 in Managua), explains clearly, long before the outbreak of fighting, that his appeal for nonviolence had not been heard by the churches of Nicaragua. He said that centuries of religious education that distorted the true meaning of the cross in Christian life had unfortunately for the time being blocked the unleashing of a true nonviolence, a popular nonviolent uprising, in Nicaragua and in Latin America generally. The current

This chapter originally appeared in slightly different form in *Grace and Power* (Orbis Books, 1987). The translation is by John Pairman Brown.

position of these brothers of ours calls nonviolence radically into question. Some reflections on our part are all the more important, for we need to know whether the historical choice to which our Nicaraguan comrades were compelled is the most strategic, the most human, and the most effective in the long term (and even in the medium term) to create a different society. Will the blow that they struck against a perverse society help or compromise an authentic struggle for liberation across Latin America? Everybody understands that the events in Nicaragua are not simply local events: they are the concretization of a line that all Christianity in Latin America will be able to take. Is it advantageous to place the peoples of Latin America on a terrain where the ruling class holds a crushing superiority in economic resources and weapons? The adversary, at one moment hesitant and indecisive (like the Carter administration in respect to Nicaragua), the next moment shows how cruel and savage its repression can be when it throws the full weight of its forces into battle, as in Guatemala and El Salvador—even though we do not believe that the Salvadoran guerrillas can be defeated by the military junta without direct intervention by the United States. Might it not be more opportune to develop, while there is still time in Latin America, other modes of envisaging the conflict? To construct other strategies?

Independently of this observation in the strategic or political realm ("What, speaking militarily, is the most efficacious stance?"), there is also a question in the ethical realm. Practically, politically, what is meant by the commandment of Jesus "Love your enemies"? What could be the theory and practice of such a conflict—or, to use church vocabulary, its theology and pastoral practice? These questions must be faced. Furthermore, I believe that ethics cannot be separated from politics and strategy. The morality of combat touches the heart of humanity; and the purity of the cause, along with the means employed to assure its triumph, is not without effect on the people's emotion. The support of the people also lies in the ethical realm. In spite of all, we see that very clearly in France, where an old socialist tradition, antedating Marx, has claimed in its own right themes—full biblical themes!—such as sharing, justice, and respect for human rights, whose moral meaning has a strong effect on people. A cold conduct of affairs is not enough to elicit popular support. Technocracy, both in the West and in the East, is in the course of showing its limitations.

A THEOLOGICAL APPROACH TO THE POLITICAL QUESTION

There are many ways to approach the preceding question or questions: political, economic, psychological, military. I believe that the theological approach, though certainly not exclusive, is nevertheless fundamental, and that no society in the process of overcoming domination (that is, oppression from whatever source) will be correctly formed if the religious dimension is neglected.

Economic or Political Level?

Generally the thinkers who wish to remodel societies focus either on the economic function or the political function. Either: How to recognize production and the manner of working? or: What kind of state? Marx devoted himself to studying the economic question: his sociology is just a part of his political economy. Hegel, more profound than Marx in my opinion, sees in the political realm the true point of entry for social change—or, speaking even more radically, for nothing more or less than human change. Hegel believed in an Absolute Spirit, hidden in the heart of the world, which like every spiritual reality tends to perfection without limit. According to him, the organized emergence of the Absolute Spirit with all its parts in our epoch would happen on the level of the state: that is, in the specific place where conflicts are conducted and resolved. The political art of savoir-vivre in the resolution of conflicts is then for our times the key virtue, the fundamental skill. For that is what allows us to arrive at a higher social synthesis, a new society. If Hegel is right over against Marx—and everything leads me to believe that he is right—the political realm, in our days, would be a privileged place where the Spirit breathes, because it is the place where the Spirit emerges. The crossroads of humanity and divinity simultaneously demand and produce political saints. Can one not say that in the person of Gandhi and Martin Luther King, for example, such have begun to show themselves? Other epochs raised up saints of a different type. It is not absurd to say that today sanctity is concentrated in the political realm in a special and original manner. That realm must then be worthy of the age.

That is why, in this domain, Christianity, especially in Latin America, has a fundamental word to speak. Our fear is that once again it will be courageous but still incomplete; that it will not have reached the final point of its intuition. Is it not the case that at present Christianity in effect has recourse to physical force, to armed violence (even though as in Nicaragua as a last resort and without brutality) to topple the mighty ones from their throne? But, is not force the weapon that the mighty ones of this world use when they have nothing better to propose? Our perception is that the raison d'être of Christianity is something different. It is, rather, to make possible the entry of grace into this world, to graft it into the heart of history. Hence there arises a mysterious dialectic between grace and power, which I wish to study insofar as possible in these few pages. I have chosen this way of posing the question in order to ask our comrades in Nicaragua: What is the force that will lead the Latin American peoples to "socialization" in the true sense of the word—that is, to communal sharing of their human and material resources in the economic, ideological, and political realms?

GRACE AND POWER

I do not think that the force that will lead those peoples to community can be power, even the revolutionary power of the proletariat, because at the end of the day power always exists as something *outside* the human being. *No power in the world can persuade me, in my heart of hearts, to give, to give myself.* At the root of oneself rests an unassailable will to autonomy. And that is as it should be. For this irreducible autonomy over against the other makes one different, "distant," from that other one. And it is nothing other than that difference and distance which permits love. I—speaking personally—could never love somebody who melted or dissolved in me, but I can love somebody who faces me and whom I face. All the attempts to make one's own self abdicate—for example, to submit itself to a discipline imposed by the building of socialism—rebound into bureaucratic, totalitarian, or dictatorial societies where all the best of socialism evaporates.

If any other doubt that, we strongly recommend that they submit themselves to some mini-experiences of socialization: for example, possessing in common a car, a house, or a television set. How difficult it is to possess things in common! How low the level of socialist consciousness really is, even among the vanguard of the working class. Only with great difficulty will persons submit themselves to a communal discipline freely accepted, will they arrive at consensus on the criteria of usage. That is why, at least in the beginning, groups who live a communal life undergo many crises and setbacks: the car breaks down and nobody, or almost nobody, is willing to take responsibility for repairs; the telephone bill soars to the stratosphere; the cupboards are dirty, the ashes are never emptied. The group tries to react and then it "produces" rules, laws, decrees. Once again *law prevails over grace.* The old story of the Bible begins again: covenant with God, of course, and guarantee of the Promised Land; but so that the people should not fall back into idolatry (for persons make their gods after their own manner and live their own lives as they decide), Moses is obliged to decree the law of the Ten Commandments, and a whole code (Leviticus) of community life appears. Once again in the bureaucratization of the revolution, Moses turns back the progress made by Jeremiah and Ezekiel, who announce (Jer. 31; Ezek. 34) the arrival of an epoch where the law will be inscribed by God on the heart of the human being. It will no longer be "exterior" to the human being. For just so far as law is conceived of as superior to the Spirit, bureaucracy and oppression will return to lord it over the Spirit, even in the interior of progressive revolutions.

In spite of these laws and rules of socialist or communal living, each one picks and chooses among them, even those who consider themselves the avant-garde of the proletariat: hence arise dachas, privileges, perquisites. It might even happen that the most advanced militants engage (at a low figure) the services of one of the "lumpen-proletariat" (perhaps a black house-cleaner) to tidy what they have made dirty: the socialist leaders are no longer there in order to serve.

Afterward, little by little, things get better. What helps in overcoming the initial crisis is the strong friendship that unites the members of the group and the immense hope aroused by the project of a new society, a new world to be constructed. What impresses everybody who goes to Nicaragua is the popular joy, joy at being harnessed all together to the task of building a new world. What changed persons, at the end of the day, was not any law, any external power, but friendship, a vision intimately lived in common, a love. This revolutionary comradeship is the only true force that can help in dealing with the criticisms, the inevitable failures in an enterprise of this sort, during this concrete apprenticeship of the socialist life. The grandeur of the cause exercises a further attraction, at least on the first revolutionary generation.

At the beginning of the experience, no persons submit themselves to communal disciplines, because there has not been born at the root of anybody's being the conviction that one must so submit oneself. In the first place it is a simple lack of experience. But also, it seems to me, there is a lack of generosity. Will the French truly have the civic generosity of their socialism, which has made all the Third World vibrate with hope? Probably not! Are the different social categories ready for sacrifice? One must confess that inside the head of each proletarian is a petty bourgeois who is not slow to make its appearance. Marx said correctly that the ruling ideas are the ideas of the ruling class. It has been a long time now that French and American workers have been living in a capitalist society. But we do not think that this sociological explanation is sufficient. The egotism of each one does not come solely from an ideology of the ruling class or system injected into the head of the ruled. In my own mind I judge that the evil is more serious. For until now nobody has succeeded in bringing about a revolutionary organization, truly born from the "base," truly traversed by a creative spirit, strong enough to destroy the social structures of oppression, the mental scaffolding of egotism plain and simple, which lead to the desire of exploiting the other or at least of reclining supinely on the other.

No "political" reeducation, at least until now, has succeeded in seriously correcting this mysterious deviation of the human race. But, in my opinion, there will be no increase of the revolutionary movement or reinforcement of a communal society until each individual participating in this social change remains convinced in the most intimate heart of his or her subjectivity that it is worth the trouble to subject oneself to the freely accepted demands of a common life and initiative. Here finally we stumble on the existence of a factor, which for want of a better word we call "grace."

What is grace but the free and spontaneous opening of one person to another—that is, to what is different from the self? It is an inspiration, poetic if you will, which convinces the heart of each person to trust the self to a social organism that transcends the self, even though one is an operative part of that social organism, and to assure its functioning. Grace is a gift that persuades one person to trust another. *From trust, unity is born. Unity in turn permits organization.* In this sense grace is opposed to power, for grace neither commands nor organizes, but inspires. Power is not the *cause* of sharing even though in the end it alone can organize sharing. Power is not the source of sharing, but the means put to its service. Grace is the only cause of this immense upsurge that leads people to put things in common; it convinces persons in the depth of their heart to give, to give themselves, to collaborate freely in a great social structure, to submit to civic disciplines.

Like power, grace has then a political function that we must rediscover: its effect is to permit, or rather, to help human beings to aspire to communal life in a society of sharing. By touching the heart of each one's subjectivity, it alone can conquer egotism at its root.

We were just speaking of political reeducation. Why have there been such monstrous deviations in the reeducation camps in the various socialist countries: the psychiatric clinics of the Soviet Union, the gulags, the Cambodian work camp . . . ? Behind these deviations must lie a perversion in theory: entrusting to a psychological or political institution (boring meetings on political reeducation, long hours of criticism and self-criticism) a task that belongs only to grace. In this realm the political philosophy of Hegel, the economic theory of Marx, the science of Freud and Reich are inadequate. Neither the state, nor a transfer of the means of production to all and for all, nor the analysis of the unconscious can open up human beings to the depths of their subjectivity and heal them, so as to become capable of a harmonious social life. Another "instrument" is needed to refashion "souls"—that is, the profound psychology of the individual: there is also a psychoanalysis conducted by the Holy Spirit.

Hence I believe that there is a subtle and complex dialectic between grace and power. Both are necessary, but without confusion or separation. It strikes me that there is as yet very little awareness of this dialectic, perhaps because theologies of liberation still lack an approach to human interiority and a more extensive theology of the Trinity. As for European theologies, they do not adequately possess the practice of life with the poor; and in consequence they do not perceive that the marginalization and the exclusion from society of millions of human beings by misery of every sort is also a trinitarian scandal! Is not the Trinity a society of three persons who are neither confused nor separated? And what is the Third World (or what we may call the Fourth World—those rejected from advanced industrial societies) but the mass of those human beings who have been either absorbed or exploited (confounded) or isolated and marginalized (separated) by a system gone mad? Apart from the question of a more systematic theology hidden behind this problem, we can look with a more attentive eye at the way Jesus acts in the gospel, and draw from this observation precious teachings for our political activity.

THE POLITICAL STATE OF GRACE

Certain points are clear. Jesus came to proclaim his kingdom, which must be sketched out in the communal societies that we desire. What does he actually say? To create the kingdom, neither power, nor possessions, nor knowledge suffice. Even if the economy is going well and bread is in abundance; even if the kingdoms of the world are able to set on its feet a planetary authority and to organize themselves better; even if science and official ideology make miraculous leaps ahead to the extent of seducing the human masses — all that is inadequate for the birth of a harmonious relationship among human beings. The reader has recognized in my description the three temptations of Jesus: to change stones into bread; to receive the homage of all the kingdoms of the earth; to conquer by a miracle the place where the national ideology is formed, the temple of Jerusalem (Matt. 4:1–11). To get on his side the scientists, intellectuals, and priests! Today Marx suggests that the secret of human happiness lies in the rectification of economic relations. Freud reveals to us the abyss of the unconscious and shows that each of us contains a sexual and emotional repression, caused by a distorted image of the father implanted in us by a patriarchal society. Reich makes a synthesis of the two: he abandons Freud's individualism and assumes Marx's socialism; according to him, society as a whole locks around our necks an iron collar of character, which must be broken.

I am far from wishing to reject the substantial scientific (or better, rational) contribution of these great men. Still we have to say that Jesus' good news is something different. It may very well presume this or that scientific truth, but it says something different in its own name. It says, at the end of the day, that in order to be happy the human being must once again enter into relation with its deepest root, which is a divine root. The axis around which the kingdom of God is constructed is an interior and communal act that has consequences in all domains, including the social and the scientific. This act consists in the opening of each one of us, in union with the others, to the Father as Jesus has revealed him. Here we need to repeat some thought on the Trinity: inasmuch as God is not Father alone, but also Brother and Spirit, this opening to God contains nothing oppressive about it. For Christians, only openness to God and God's grace can convince each person to give, and to give self: this is undoubtedly one of the high points of Jesus' preaching, the "hidden treasure" of his thought, which few know how to find. Only the creator can attain the root of the being that the creator has created. No exterior constraint or intervention — neither power, nor organization, nor psychoanalytic cure — can be substituted for the free intervention of grace. And even the knowledge of God does not depend on human strength: "Nobody knows the Father except the Son, and that person to whom the Son wishes to reveal him" (Luke 10:22). Faith is necessary to receive the gift of grace and with it the strength of individual and social sharing. We must have faith: that is, we must ask the Son that we may *know* the Father and thereby live out the trinitarian harmony among earthly realities. In biblical language, to "know" means to have a strong and organic vital relationship with the one loved.

That has important political consequences. It means that revolutionaries must proceed, with full awareness, in search of grace so that the revolution will not be aborted—will not fall into reformism, or terror, or bureaucracy. It is impossible for us to restrict ourselves to placing our confidence in any revolutionary organization, however excellent it may be, if we wish to remain open to that grace, for, *by definition, grace escapes from every mold fashioned to retain it.* It is possible and necessary to have an "inspired" political power, but the secret of inspiration is somewhere else.

In this sense the current demands of many leftist movements in the world—no less in Poland than in Latin America—are indeed interesting: for them, "autonomy," "self-management" (*autogestão*) completes and balances the socialization of the means of production. Autonomy means that every individual, every entity, has a life and creativity of its own, which cannot be expressed solely through a larger grouping. For example, the trade union expresses an aspect of the working class that is not necessarily represented in the workers' party. Hence it is not proper for the union to be absorbed by the party. So each person is autonomous as an individual; and though each has the duty of remaining united with the other members of the group and submitting to a social discipline, that does not mean that any should abdicate personal creativity or be obliged to obey without the right of protest and refusal. That comes down in the end to saying that communal inspiration is not produced through the organizations that are animated by it.

To return to the great men who inspired the political reflection of the past century and a half, we could summarize in the following manner. Marx was obsessed by the question of economic institutions and did not see correctly the question of the state and of power. Hegel perhaps laid the theoretical foundations of totalitarianism, for he makes of the state a kind of God, the place where the absolute Spirit emerges.

In Christian thought, the Spirit comes from elsewhere, from a *different* place: "the spirit blows where it wishes . . ., you do not know where it comes from nor where it is going" (John 3:8). It is this difference, this "elsewhere" of grace on which nobody can put a hand, that nobody can reduce or possess, and that constitutes the *theoretical* basis of the autonomy and self-management of individuals and of groups. For what they most deeply *are* does not arise from human strength. Therefore we cannot absolutely define or control it. There, it seems to this writer, is an important contribution of theological reflection for current political thought. For at bottom, it is monism, whether of spirit or of matter, that lies at the origin of all totalitarianisms.

GRACE AND EXPLICIT FAITH: POWER AS SERVICE

The gospel shows us that the search for grace does not depend solely on explicit faith: for the love of the poor, of the wretched, the sacrament constituted by a brother or a sister in need, is already a real relationship to Christ and to his grace. "I was naked and you clothed me, I was hungry and you gave me to eat—to me the Christ!" "But when did I do that? I didn't even know you, I didn't believe in you." "Each time that you acted so to one of the least of my brethren, it was to me that you did it" (Matt. 25). It is love that will judge us. Still, implicit faith, like any unconscious state, is an abnormal state. We must become conscious of the divine dimension of being. That is the task of evangelization when it is at its most authentic.

In the end, in a theological perspective, provided we resolutely avoid reductionist tendencies, which limit evangelization to the political realm, provisionally we may say that the new societies are sketches of the kingdom of God. But we must never forget: the kingdom of God is *of God*. Without God these "attempts" cannot even be tried, indispensable as they are to demonstrate by seeing that paradise is possible. Hope is nourished by concrete realizations.

Once we have accepted this fundamental datum of a radically different pole from which grace drops down like the morning dew, without difficulty power becomes situated in its proper place. Jesus in no way rejects political power. The apostle Paul requires that Christians should be subject to it, for authority is an order established by God (Rom. 13:2), an instrument of God (Rom. 13:4) to establish justice and punish the evildoer. Precisely on that account, then, it is necessary that public powers should correspond to the order established by God and should effectively help human beings to do good. Jesus, far from rejecting power as a means for installing the kingdom, on the contrary insists that it should be at the service of the kingdom. The concept of power in the gospel is markedly original. Jesus flees to the mountain when the multitudes wish to seize him to make him a king (John 6:15), for he refuses to be divinized in that manner, in the aspect of political authority as in his third temptation, as if that would constitute the ultimate response to the problem of humanity. But on the other hand, Jesus recognizes and encourages the value of *power as service*, which is not the cause of sharing, but which organizes it. Thus, *after* the multiplication of the loaves, he makes the hungry crowds sit down in groups of fifty or a hundred (Mark 6:40). He suggests to authorities of every type that they should be inspired by his attitude: "You call me Teacher and Lord, and you speak well, for so I am. If I, then, your Lord and Teacher, have washed your feet, then you also should wash each other's feet" (John 16:13–14). "Let whoever wishes to be first among you become the servant of all" (Mark 10:44).

THE STRUGGLE OF JESUS, OR THE STRUGGLE OF GRACE

But still this attitude of Jesus was never clearly understood, either by the ordinary people or by his own disciples. *Yesterday, as today, the supremacy of grace over force seems unacceptable.* When Jesus began to explain that in order to live out this mysterious dialectic of the kingdom and to receive what power could not give—namely, grace—people had to be fed by his example, his inspiration, his word, his ideas, and even with his whole being, his body and blood—at this point, the scandal was too great and tripped up even the best. The circle of his friends began to disintegrate. We naturally ask: What happens to an authentic revolutionary when the people abandon him, when the people's ramparts around him crumble? Because his presence is intolerable for those who profit from the privileges of the established order, the mailed fist of the ruling classes seizes him, on the grounds that thereafter they will have nothing to fear. Several times in the gospel we read of attempts at assassination of Jesus, or attempts to get rid of him; but at the beginning he was always surrounded by so many persons that these attempts came to nothing (conflict with his family, Mark 3:20–21, 31–32; with religious readers, Mark 11:28–32; attempts at assassination, Mark 11:18; 14:1–21; John 7:32, 45–48, and especially at Nazareth, Luke 4:28–29). Finally the attempts succeed at Gethsemane, where Jesus is found alone with a few sleeping apostles around him.

THE "CRITICAL" FUNCTION OF GRACE

This dialectic between grace and power, and this supremacy of grace over power, are the reasons why, in an evangelical perspective, it is impossible to idolize the state, to make of it an absolute. Openness to that grace, which alone allows communion and participation and which comes from elsewhere, means that, at every instant, power is relativized as a final solution of the problems that arise. But it is not sufficient to hold this fundamental position of not turning power into an absolute. We must also draw its practical consequences for the political life of the societies of sharing, which we are seeking. Here again I take a theological approach. What we need is to create social structures in which power rests solely in rules of service, where the administrator washes the feet of those administered. We must set in place a social disposition such that at every instant power can be brought down from its throne, while at the same time enjoying the respect and authority without which it cannot play its role. I take the word "authority" (Latin *auctoritas*) in its etymological sense, "that which makes something 'increase'"

(Latin *augeo*). Power has as its function to make the living forces of society increase around it.

What is the place where the Spirit of God breathes with greatest intensity? Certainly among its people of the poor, the little ones, the humble of the earth. "Blessed are the poor" as we saw does not mean "Long live poverty, misery, exploitation"; but that those ones are happy who, precisely because of poverty, must share to survive. Among the inhabitants of a *favela*, earth, water, and light are already socialized because each one draws water from the same well or faucet, because the lines for electric lights pass from one hut to another, because the earth is by necessity common property (the land is squatter territory where nobody has property rights). For those crowded together in a prison cell, whoever holds something for exclusive use becomes an intolerable burden on the others and will either be bodily expelled or assassinated. Extreme necessity gives birth to either heaven or hell. Heaven, if each one, going beyond self, arrives at a marvelous equilibrium, due to an immense respect for the neighbor; each halts barefoot before the doorway of the other's intimacy and strives to offer and receive from the other all that one has and all that one is. Hell, if even one person arrogates permission to use, in however slight a degree, force and deception to survive. We said that God is love, and that God moves in love as the birds fly and the fish swim in love. That is why atheism, before being a theoretical problem, is a practical problem. In a place where there is no love or sharing, God cannot be present. The prophet Ezekiel relates that he saw the glory of God (that is, God's presence) leave Jerusalem (Ezek. 10–11). That is what happens in societies of nonsharing and nonlove.

Societies that totalize power within the hands of certain persons and that capitalize wealth are necessarily and by essence atheistic. Or perhaps better, idolatrous. In the place of the true God another absolute is placed: the party, science, wealth. That is why the wretched outskirts of São Paulo, or of other big cities of the world, in spite of the crimes for which they are the theater (murders, thefts, drug use) are more *religious* than the middle-class houses, for in extreme poverty sharing has again become possible. There one cannot avoid seeing the misery of the neighbor, one cannot refuse the other a dish of food if one has it.

God has less difficulty in operating here than elsewhere (in truth there are very few places in the world where God feels fully "at ease," so great is human egotism). It is then for this *theological* reason and not for a political one that power must be approached from the base: the mayor, the general, the bishop, the priest, the one responsible for a zone must go to the *favela* and not it to them, for it is in these places that the Spirit of God breathes.

The ancients said: *Vox populi, vox dei.* Strictly speaking, the voice of the poor and the humble is the voice of God; the people may lose their senses and demand the release of Barabbas rather than the release of Jesus. But it is with a sound instinct that the Nicaraguan radio repeats that the voice of the people is the voice of God. Power must at all costs stay in contact with this critical place, which in turn criticizes it. Here the voice of true reason, of the uncreated Wisdom, makes itself heard most plainly, with the fewest parasitical attachments, through the mouth of the poor. Then power will avoid the temptation to escape from the earth that saw its birth and from the people that it must serve; it will avoid the disaster of becoming a god, it will be called back to order, it will be comforted by the tenderness of the poor, it will see the true problems. When one enters into contact with the living God, wherever God is to be found, the idols fall from their thrones.

A "political state of grace" (a phrase used by French journalists during the first months of the Mitterrand government) should truly mean a society where power has not been monopolized by a minority and where social changes are such that the functioning of society comes more from a spirit infusing the people than from laws (in the sense of Montesquieu). Such a political state of grace is born in a society when in principle the people do not delegate power to anybody, but entrust limited tasks to public servants. Hence the importance of these new forms of organization for which people are searching: the factory commission, which takes on the administration together with other social partners; the delegate of the street elected by the inhabitants, the assemblies of the quarter; general assemblies of workers in the factories or in agricultural enterprises; a change in the manner of naming bishops who, until now, come down from on high, are more chosen by the groups who direct the church and from among their own number than indicated by the people; the autonomy of regions delineated by history, the decentralization of power; and finally, the emplacement of vital interests of populations on the world level and acceptance of an international mediating power (which will result inevitably in limitations on national sovereignty).

Why is there so much money in the hands of those who have oil or technology, and so little in the hands of others? The earth is for all human beings, it must be repeated. It does not belong solely to Saudi Arabia or to the industrially advanced countries; there are no exclusive property rights, either over goods or over the products of intelligence.

Evidently, to build these new forms of organization presupposes many sacrifices among all, a very great civic generosity. The living standard of most social categories in the First World must be frozen or perhaps reduced if the powers in place are really to start from the genuine needs of the great majority of human beings on this planet. It is not certain that we are ready for that! The political state of grace is perhaps very far off. In any case, a shift in power of itself does not suffice to create it, as we have said a thousand times.

Now we turn to the Christians who, on the one hand, have been forced into the use of violence because their struggle has remained isolated without adequate external support; and to those, on the other hand, who believe that violence is inevitable, in some sense a necessary evil, the lesser of two evils; and even to those who think that legitimate defense by force of arms is a Christian theology. Have we been too far away to help you create alternatives, you who have taken up arms? Did we help you enough when the time came? The fact of revolutionary violence is simply there, and each of us is involved in it. Mahatma Gandhi said that it is better to be violent than passive if, unfortunately, one does not know how to create in advance, both in oneself and in society, a nonviolent mode of struggle.

But we cannot refrain from asking an even more serious question. When we overcome power by force, are we not allowing power to be what Jesus wished it never to be: the ultimate recourse to escape from a situation devoid of grace? Could there not have been in this attitude a fatal germ of mistrust with regard to grace? That is what leads us to ask ourselves: Can the most profound and original part of Christianity continue to spawn revolutions in the Third World if it does not take more seriously the alternative of nonviolence?

Another serious question also comes to mind. To solve a problem, the first condition is to state it correctly. Is it not the case that we can no longer content ourselves with an individual nonviolence solely on the level of little, interpersonal conflicts? In fact, and this is the whole point, we must pass from a nonviolence on the level of persons to a nonviolence on the level of states. It is a question of life and death for all humanity.

As for ourselves, we have made the choice of active nonviolence as a method and mystique of combat. To speak the truth, we do not think that there is currently in Latin America an intellectual or spiritual environment sufficient for the message of nonviolence to be heard adequately by the churches. Miguel d'Escoto has spoken excellently on this subject in the article cited above. But we hope that things are in the process of changing. Perhaps we have not worked out in sufficient depth — above all in practice, but also in theory, in the theology of liberation — what the specific effectiveness of the kingdom of God might be. *There is yet to be found a theology and a pastoral practice of conflict*, and with it an organization of the popular movement on the continental and international level along such lines that civil disobedience would become irresistible. Perhaps our Latin American church has not yet sufficiently perceived that its people already know how to struggle to throw off the yoke of injustice in the manner of the Suffering Servant of whom the prophet Isaiah speaks in his fifty-third chapter.

Chapter 10

Why Active Nonviolence in Brazil?

The word "nonviolence" is unpleasant to the ear, because it seems to denote disincarnate idealism, passivity, or low-grade pacifism. Those who have studied the matter know that it is none of these. Nonviolence is an original mode of struggle, of dealing with conflict. It is realistic because it recognizes that conflict exists, that human history is woven out of it. It is creative because it dares to claim that inflicting death is not necessarily a genuine mode of combat at all. One can be "human" in battle even against human beings who have become wild beasts. Nonviolence is not a discovery of yesterday. It is found at all ages, in almost all civilizations, among many peoples. In our age it was popularized by Mahatma Gandhi and Martin Luther King, Jr. We approach this matter from three different viewpoints: the psychological, the socio-political, and the theological.

THE PSYCHOLOGICAL APPROACH

The psychology of conflict has its own rules; and understanding them is of the highest importance in designing and implementing adequate training, and thus in preparing the strategy

---

This chapter originally appeared in *Grace and Power* (Orbis Books, 1987). The translation is by John Pairman Brown.

of victory. The reactions felt and aroused by an armed person or a group are very different from when persons are unarmed. The aggression present in both cases is not expressed in the same way. Four examples follow.

The Peasants of Alagamar

The state of Paraíba is in northeastern Brazil. Its capital is João Pessoa, its bishop at this writing Dom José-Maria Pires. There, farm workers and guards hired by a great landed proprietor have been in conflict for a long time. One day the guards tried to evict by force three hundred workers—men, women, and children—who were planting beans. These peasants had already been introduced, superficially, to nonviolence; for in this diocese for some time there has been a network of church base communities and a Center for the Defense of Human Rights. The guards arrived with their usual threats; there were ten of them, all armed to the teeth. The peasants, without saying a word, surrounded the guards; and some of the peasants, the oldest men, took the weapons out of the guards' hands and went off to give them to the police (even though the police were in cahoots with the landowner). This action of three hundred unarmed peasants, in silence approaching ten armed guards and encircling them, created an amazing psychological effect, the effect of numbers, despite the fact that the guards were heavily armed. Certainly one must be prepared for an action like this and, above all, not be afraid. But the tone must not be provocative or humiliating, and events must take place rapidly in order to use the factor of surprise.

Now imagine a different scenario. Suppose the same number of guards confront the same number of peasants, but with the difference that some of the peasants have brought their weapons "just in case," and that as tempers rise they take their weapons out. Anybody can see that the combat will change its nature, for the psychological mechanisms are no longer the same. The guards will be afraid, for they thought they were confronting unarmed persons and here are guns pointed at them. Then they will attack so as to defend themselves, or at least be prepared to fire, even though afterward the crowd will overwhelm them. Here fear is in charge.

Again, the psychological conditions that permit nonviolent struggle disappear when one or two members of the nonviolent group run away. The cowardice of a few will lead the soldiers to conclude that they have before them persons who will give in at the first shot. Neither arrogance nor cowardice, if nonviolence is to be effective.

Again, suppose the peasants are now only thirty in number and the guards remain at ten. Thirty peasants cannot easily encircle ten firm, armed men; whereas three hundred peasants determined to advance, even though without weapons, cannot all be neutralized; there is not time to kill them all if they maintain a genuine element of surprise. Thus conflict has its psychological rules, which change according to the scenario.

It is plain that the driving forces of this nonviolent confrontation are the *wisdom* to evaluate the forces that one is confronting, and the *courage* to make a calculated risk of one's life, for nonviolence is not suicide. And above all the internal disposition of wishing *neither the death nor the humiliation* of the adversary; the guards feel that neither their life nor their honor is being threatened, while they recognize that this people's force is irresistible, because it is in large number and would never retreat. We always say, *"Podemos morrer mas não vamos correr"* ("We may die but we won't run"). Active nonviolence comes from the association of two principles, force and gentleness. Starting from these psychological mechanisms, one can image a whole style of combat and, hence, a strategy.

The Strike of the Metalworkers of São Bernardo

In April and May 1980 there was a strike of forty days among the metalworkers of greater São Paulo, in particular those of the Volkswagen plant, under the leadership of the union of São Bernardo municipality, a union headed by Lula. The whole city was mobilized to support the strikers and their families. The dioceses of Santo André (under Bishop Claudio Humes) and of São Paulo were in the front lines, for the cause was just and the methods peaceful. It will be recalled that in Brazil the unions are not autonomous but subordinate to the government, as in Poland. There is no one national central workers' union as there is in France or in the United States: that is, there is no liberty of association among the different professional categories, so that a metalworker cannot belong to the same union as a bricklayer or a domestic employee. That obviously weakens the working class very much. Furthermore, there are no collective contracts. In most countries, contracts are collective: the business signs the labor contract with the totality of the professional category, and in case of a dispute it is the *representatives* of the workers who do the negotiating. In Brazil it is the court system that sits in judgment when the working contract is broken, which very much impedes the legal process. In Brazil a single worker signs an individual contract with what may be an enormous enterprise. Always there is the disproportion between an isolated worker with nothing but one person's skills in face of the enterprise that recruits the worker and has elsewhere to turn.

Add to all this that the living standard of half the population is about 10 percent that of the same group in the United States. The workers in big multinational corporations are in general better paid than most of the population. Fifty percent of Brazilian workers are at the legal minimum or less, in 1985 values $40 per month. Still it must be recognized that the workers in big corporations are the drive-wheel of the economy and that the fate of all other labor disputes hangs on the outcome of theirs.

In the strike of the municipality of São Bernardo, the churches made their parish halls available for meetings and for collection and storage of food for the families of the strikers. When the police first blocked off the stadium, then the public square, for general assemblies of tens of thousands of strikers, Bishop Humes opened up his cathedral, which became in a new way the house of the people. The church base communities were mobilized throughout the city to gather food in all the quarters, even the poorest. Aid from outside also was significant; international solidarity from trade unions and other sources played its role.

The strike was without violence but not in the strict sense nonviolent. By that we mean that the great majority made no conscious, principled choice of nonviolence, and that the non-violent activists played only a minor role. But they participated by safeguarding the movement of food trucks each night toward the regions that had been blocked off. This role won them the confidence of the strikers and allowed them to propose an idea for the celebration of the First of May. For that day the mass of workers determined, at whatever cost, to win back the stadium of São Bernardo where the general assemblies had been held until the police closed it. A Mass was scheduled for the first thing in the morning. At the planning meeting a typical nonviolent proposal was made. An activist from the nonviolent group of São Paulo suggested that persons coming to the Mass should carry a kilo of rice in their left hand and a flower in their right: the rice to support the strikers and the flower for the soldiers.

On the First of May the sight was unforgettable. The morning was radiant. Overhead two big helicopters with machine guns aimed at the people circled at a low altitude the towers of the crowded Cathedral of São Bernardo. The bishop presided at the liturgy. The company of soldiers surrounded the cathedral square, and two hundred thousand strikers with their families and friends encircled the soldiers. If there had been a panic, a police charge, tear-gas grenades, who knows how many persons would have been trampled in the disorder! The little children walked forward to give their flowers to the soldiers, who were quite embarrassed with this gift. Some stuck them in their rifles, some accepted them awkwardly with their heads hanging down, some hugged the children. The crowd sat down on the ground and called out friendly slogans to the soldiers: "Brother soldier, don't get into it (*não entre nessa*)! You also are exploited!"

These attitudes exercised enormous psychological pressure. Simultaneously the adversary clearly felt the "love" that was being offered them and also a force like a wave, a people's wave in action. Again: force and gentleness. The feelings of the adversary that were reached were their highest ones; the soldiers also had children. Would they fire on a child offering them flowers? That would really be an act of cowardice. Psychologically, this soldier is in a situation of inferiority. If by bad luck he should shoot, a murder of this sort would reverse public opinion and unite it against the oppressor. To move the adversary by touching the noblest and purest part of the person; to conquer the hearts of the millions of humble and poor by an attitude at once courageous, organized, and unarmed: those are the psychological secrets that make nonviolence work. Evidently this type of combat presupposes a high degree both of moral life and of organized intelligence. Much strategy, much ethics! The moral level of this struggle would have had to fall only a little, by provocation or by humiliation of the enemy from hatred in the heart, for the psychological mechanisms to be snapped, which until then made the people leap and the adversary stumble. Then the war would have fallen back into its traditional patterns: violence and murder.

We need to add that each situation demands a nonviolent response appropriate to it. What worked on May 1, 1980, might not work on May 1, 1981. The factors of society, politics, and repression change endlessly. It may happen that the brigade comes ready to kill father, mother, and children together, as is happening today in El Salvador and Guatemala. We need to study very carefully the circumstances where this or that action is to take place. Perhaps we should install movie cameras on the roofs of buildings or in secrecy to film any atrocities. In general, the tactic in the case of a hard war of nonviolent character is to *isolate the incorrigible*. In any shock troops, in any repressive state apparatus, there is bound to be a fascist core ready for anything; but this core is limited. We need to identify the fascist core so as to isolate and condemn it.

Active nonviolence requires a shrewdness that will not be spoon-fed with fairytales. Nonviolence has always had to defend itself against charges of being a naive sentimentality or a beautiful, irresponsible idealism. "Be as harmless as doves but as wise as serpents," Jesus tells us (Matt. 10:16). If goodness is all one has, one will be plucked like a pear. If one is merely prudent, one will also be cruel. The gospel is an equilibrium of opposites; so Heraclitus makes the universe out to be a "reciprocal harmony, as of the bow and the lyre." To retain these two characteristics, nonviolence must hold itself up to two exacting standards: an intense militancy so as to create a powerful people's force; and exact information about the enemy it will find itself facing. We must set up the Intelligence Service of the poor! Like a good general we must at every instant study the nature of the terrain in order to map out the response best adapted to it, and to analyze the relations of force between friends and enemies.

But now, even though we should take all precautions to avoid being killed, we have to admit that the possibility of sacrifice cannot be totally avoided. Better die than kill! However carefully our action may have been planned, an irreversible event can always occur. But when we think about it, in traditional war many die on both sides. In a nonviolent war, all those who die are on the side of the oppressed, but in much fewer numbers than in a conventional war. The people's cadres who reject violent struggle will survive in much greater numbers; when it takes ten years to train a base community and good militants, it is not intelligent to move forward to a massacre. Also the self-sacrifice of the just is a powerful appeal, able to reverse the opinion of many. Later we shall give a Brazilian example. For the meantime we can remember the sacrifice of Jesus. We recall the effect produced by the assassination of Gandhi; of Martin Luther King, Jr.; by the "disappearance" of thousands of Argentinians, which at this writing fuels the resistance of the "crazy women of [the Plaza] de Mayo." (The mothers and grandmothers of the *desaparecidos* of Argentina—who include children and infants—gather every Thursday in front of the palace of the president of the republic in the Plaza de Mayo to demonstrate their indignation. Some have paid for this heroic attitude with their lives. They go on.)

In the episode we are discussing, the body of strikers finally carried off the victory by winning back the stadium. It would take too long to describe all the details of this engagement. Let us just state that the soldiers were given the order to climb back into their personnel carriers, which they did in a hurry, with some making the V sign of victory to the excited crowd. It is also true that afterward the strikers *provisionally* lost their campaign and that repression was unleashed on their leaders. The people cannot expect immediate victory; they must be prepared for a long war.

The Fast at Crateús

In 1981 in the city of Crateús, in the state of Ceará, one of the poorest and driest of the northeast, there was a long drought and much hunger. The peasants flowed into the towns and the shopkeepers were afraid for their stores. The municipality wanted to form a committee to deal with the danger of looting. The bishop, Dom Fragoso, a nonviolent activist, expressed the opinion that it would be better to form a committee to help the hungry and not to expel them. The situation was explosive. A hungry belly has no ears, and the police were ready to shoot. A special diocesan assembly of the base communities was urgently convened. Alfredinho[1] announced his intention to carry out a public fast for eight days, drinking only water. Like Gandhi, Alfredinho invited people to pray with him morning, noon, and night. For only prayer and fasting, he said, can drive out the demons of fear and egotism (Matt. 17:21, in Latin versions). This public fast was carefully organized and publicized throughout the diocese. Alfredinho observed it in a church on the outskirts of the city and many joined him in his times of prayer. At one of them he launched Operation PAF (*Porta Aberta aos Famintos*, "Open Door to the Hungry"). Any family that wanted to open their door to the hungry to offer them what they had — shade against the sun, a glass of water, a plate of rice — would put a placard reading PAF on their front door. The victims would know by that that they would receive a fraternal welcome: no need for fear or shame. Several thousand homes, often very poor, blossomed out in placards; the bishop's house was the first. The city's atmosphere totally changed. What little the people had was shared, the multiplication of loaves was seen again. On the eighth day the fast ended with a downpour of rain! The people organized a great procession of thanksgiving.

The Death of José Silvino Valdevino

All that we set down here comes from the November 9, 1981, report of the regional Coordination for Gospel Nonviolence of the diocese of João Pessoa in the state of Paraíba.

José was murdered with six bullets in his body on October 7,

1981, at Salamargo near the *fazenda* (plantation) Ana-Cláudia in the municipality of Espírito Santo, Paraíba. He was forty-nine years old and left nine children, five of them under twenty-one. He was murdered by the *capataz* (overseer) of the *fazenda*, Manuel Batista. Ten families besides José's were always being threatened with eviction. Together they had been farming 42 hectares where they were living for more than five years. The perpetrator of the crime, following the orders of the proprietor of the *fazenda*, had destroyed José Silvino's hut with a bulldozer a month before. Then, with a group of hired guards, he had begun to move in, forcibly, on the neighbors' fields and plant sugarcane (which is also processed to provide alcohol as motor fuel). The crime was committed at 6:00 in the morning, the police were notified at 7:30; by noon they had still not arrived on the scene, either to establish the facts or to protect the other farmers, who were also being threatened with death. They had just twenty kilometers to drive.

Here are the facts in order, as determined by the Coordination for Gospel Nonviolence:

Manuel Aureliano, a big *latifundiário* (landed proprietor) tries to evict eleven families living on land they call their own and where they have been farming for five years. José Silvino has been to the official surveyor's office and has in his possession a certificate that these lands do not belong to Manuel Aureliano. For five years no other person has put in an appearance to claim these lands.

On the fifth of October the eleven families peacefully resist an invasion directed by the *capataz* with four *pistoleiros* (gunmen) and four tractors to destroy the peasants' crops.

On the sixth of October, still being threatened with death, the peasants address a letter to the president of the republic then in office, Aureliano Chaves, as well as to various local officials.

On the seventh of October, at six o'clock in the morning, Manuel Batista arrives at the site where José Silvino is working. He jumps out of his car and says, "You son of a bitch, you have no business being here. Are you setting yourself up as some kind of lawyer?" José Silvino: "No, I am not the lawyer." The *capataz* says, "I'm going to shoot you now." José Silvino: "*Estou aqui com minha vida para viver ou para morrer* (I'm here with my life to live or to die)." Then the *capataz* takes out his revolver and José Silvino falls dead with six bullets in his body.

After the crime, Manuel Batista stayed more than four hours on the scene threatening to kill three other workers. Witnesses testified that the guards, armed with rifles and 38-gauge revolvers, said, "This is to teach you never to encourage people to plant on this land."

The widow of José Silvino, when she came back from her husband's funeral, said, "Now more than ever we will not leave this land."

Seven days after the death of José Silvino, his comrades attended the Mass for him and with him, and spontaneously offered these prayers:

"Let this blood become seed, grow, and give us courage for the struggle."

"Comrade José, your blood is here and gives us courage."

"Another time Jesus was crucified and they said, 'If he is the Son of God, may God let the blood of this just man fall on us.'[2] And so in this holy Mass we ask that the blood of our brother José Silvino should stay with us as our light and our road so that we can all advance."

"The blood of Jesus spilled on the ground did not stop its work there. From it will grow a tree big enough for the birds of the air to nest in its branches. I ask that all the workers and farmers present here should unite themselves in prayer and in the action of that fighter and struggler, José Silvino our brother, who died for justice."

The Coordination, which prepared this text (which we have summarized above) and sent it out to the communities, ends its report with two questions.

1. What are the elements of violence that we can observe in the attitudes of those in power?

2. In the face of violence, what attitudes, what routes are open to farmers to direct the conflict so that they may resist violence (in themselves, in others, and in their adversaries) and remain on the land?

THE SOCIO-POLITICAL APPROACH

In the second half of the twentieth century, we consider that the nature of social conflict has been totally changed. If it were not shocking to so speak, one might say that it had taken a quantum leap upward! The concentration of wealth and of the means of production in the hands of the ruling class has been accompanied by a parallel concentration of the means of repression in the same circles. Therefore *it is not strategically advantageous for the poor to confront the powerful and rich on the terrain of the latter with* their *weapons.* The example of the Nicaraguan revolution might seem to prove the contrary. But we shall maintain that its circumstances have been quite exceptional. On the principle that "the exception proves the rule," we shall suggest that in other cases, like that of El Salvador, where its exceptional circumstances are not found, the general principle that we propose is valid.

In Nicaragua, the United States during the Carter administration was hesitant about extending full support to the dictator Anastasio Somoza. Later we shall suggest certain reasons. Here we may recall that during this epoch there was an effort at world control of the economy by North America, Japan, and Europe, the Trilateral Commission. From this source came a policy of "opening" in Latin America, orchestrated through the human-rights campaign, to win back a part of public opinion on that continent, to prevent the steamboilers of many lands there from exploding. But as soon as Ronald Reagan came to the presidency, this policy was reversed. The American people, humiliated by the defeats of President Carter in Iran, for example, but still hesitant (for Reagan was elected by only a minority of the electorate, with many abstentions), brought into power a man determined to repress any desire for independence on the part of countries that might have been contaminated by Cuba: that was the big fear. And so we have come to see what repression undertaken by great powers is capable of when it is unleashed, even if only at second hand.

Until recently a school for torture was maintained in Panama, which trained the military of the entire Latin American continent. In El Salvador women and children were decapitated; girls were murdered, with the heads of their fiancés sewn into their bellies. We may have seen the brainwashing of an American Jesuit in Guatemala who, two months after he disappeared, was shown on television confessing his "errors." In Guatemala there have been cases of cannibalism — soldiers eating the brains of children whose heads had been dashed to the ground in front of their mothers. [All this I have verified personally or from the most responsible sources. D.B.] In El Salvador there have been 30,000 deaths in less than three years, and 500,000 refugees; eleven priests and one bishop have been murdered in two years; there have been abominable cases of torture; death squadrons function openly. In short: a terror campaign to destroy support for the guerrillas, in a population of 5 million where fourteen families possess 85 percent of the land. At this writing everybody wants to negotiate except the United States administration.

To repeat, in the form of a question: Is it strategically advantageous for the poor to confront the powerful with *their* weapons?

Everybody knows that the only reason the United States Marines are not already in Cuba, Nicaragua, El Salvador, Guatemala is the pressure exerted both internationally and also within the United States. We have not fully recognized the extent to which the 1970s were marked by an extraordinary proliferation of base groups: not merely the church base communities of Latin America that we have discussed, but also in North America. North American Christianity is in the process of waking up. It is of great importance to link together the networks engaged in nonviolent struggle in Europe, Latin America, and North America; much effort during the last few years has gone into this. Many nations beyond Latin America are opposed to North American intervention out of fear of a major conflict. All this simply goes to show that weapons other than bombs and guns are effective in holding back repression, *on the condition that people become organized.* It is popular pressure that is decisive, and not primarily summit conversations.

The industrialized nations have partially learned one lesson. If for forty years there has been no world war, it is not out of humanitarianism but because the destruction is unthinkable, and victor and vanquished would alike be vanquished. (That is not to say that we should count on the policy of "deterrence" to maintain the peace indefinitely, for the nuclear powers are driven by demonic powers beyond their control, and are constantly taking greater and greater risks for the sake of imagined strategic advantages.) Should it be assumed that the poor are even less motivated by intelligence and prudence than the rich? Why should they take up weapons for their liberation, while the powerful with all their ambivalence take some precautions not to arrive at that point? Gandhi had perceived, intuitively more than rationally, this shift in the nature of conflict, when he confronted England, the greatest industrial power of his time. He must somehow have felt this concentration of the means of repression, which has been made possible by the age of the machine.

It is often said that Gandhi was facing "civilized" people, the British, and further that he settled only the problem of his country's colonial status, not its poverty. People say, "where are his disciples? Who was there to maintain the continuity of his action after his death? The future of nations must not depend on charismatic leaders; strategies cannot be built on any such unreliable basis." We may say that Gandhi was a forerunner of surpassing genius. He realized that new methods of combat must be systematized and adapted to the industrial age. Just as Lenin brought into reality only a most imperfect sketch of a socialist society in a backward industrial country, so Gandhi only opened the door for a new manner of "living out" conflict in industrial society. The one was an innovator in the realm of social models, the other in that of modes of combat. It is sectarian to put one on a pedestal and disqualify the other. That denies our political culture. All passion blinds the intelligence.

It might be useful to distinguish two types of combat: conventional wars between nations, and people's struggles for liberation. I am concerned here with the second.

The idea proposed here is a very simple one: never to station oneself on the adversary's terrain by making use of weapons that kill; but, rather, to multiply base groups and help people move step by step to massive and organized civil disobedience. There is a whole scheme of escalation in nonviolence: after dialogue, publication of the truth, and popular pressure prove insufficient, the ultimate weapon remains—total paralysis of the country, a general strike. No government, even if armed to the teeth, can for long control a nation against 95 percent of its people. We saw that very well in Iran, where, in the first phase, the people confronted with their bare hands the army of the Shah, one of the most powerful in the world. It cannot be said that the revolution itself in Iran was nonviolent! Its mystique, unfortunately, was quite the reverse. But Islam is capable of quite a different mystique from the "integrist"—really "totalitarian"—one of Khomeini. Still we can say that during that first period, the revolution in Iran was unarmed.

We know further that it is not necessary to organize 95 percent of the population in base communities. All that is needed is an adequate number, perhaps thousands, of small, popular cadres, on the level of the street or the village, coming out of these communities and trained by their "pastorate" or ideology, in order to orient the population at-large and coordinate its actions. We may give as examples, without making any judgment on their ideology or goals, the French militants of Lip (the watch factory where a strike brought in self-management for a while), the kibbutzim in Israel, communist parties in countries that accept or tolerate them, the mullahs in Iran.

For such cadres to come into being presupposes intense militant activity. Cadres with a principled commitment to nonviolence require the most training of all, for it cannot be improvised; it is nothing less than a *spirituality united to an organization*.

Now let us analyze the people's insurrection in Nicaragua. We still do not have adequate information or analysis to draw up a full summation. But it would certainly be at least questionable to claim that, among all the factors working in favor of the insurrection, armed force was the principal one. For a number of years the Frente Sandinista tried without success to get the population to rise up. The first insurrection was a disaster. In fact, what played the decisive role in getting the masses to move was the murder of two innocent journalists: Pedro Chamorro, and the North American reporter Bill Stewart, killed in the middle of the revolution in front of the television cameras of the whole world. Pedro Chamorro was editor of an important liberal newspaper. His summary execution by Somoza brought over into the active opposition a large part of the middle class and intellectuals. Also it must not be forgotten that Somoza had shamefully appropriated for his own benefit the international aid that had poured in after the earthquake that destroyed Managua in 1972: another motive for the people's anger.

Furthermore, the church for some years had been playing an important role: orienting and defending the people; making public protest against the abuses of the government; above all, beginning to create those base communities that are the great force by which the peoples of Latin America are organized. (The base communities of Nicaragua began some time after those in Brazil, and developed especially after the insurrection. The popular revolution in Nicaragua came about with the massive support of Christians—without their having been organized in base communities.) Finally, the second insurrection broke out. When the American journalist died before the eyes of the whole world, indignation exceeded all bounds. Somoza could no longer cover up the savage character of his regime. North American public opinion turned, as one person, from Somoza. The Carter administration, still vacillating, found it impossible to continue its aid to the dictator's regime. *The death of the innocent when seen around the world was a terrible weapon against the dictator.*

In all these facts we can see in cameo the characteristics of a nonviolent action—or, if we prefer, the nonviolent dimensions of every insurrectional struggle, when it is really the poor who move into action. Finally—and we end this brief analysis of the people's revolt in Nicaragua with this very specific feature—there was a real will for nonviolence on the part of the comrades most responsible for the revolution. We should not forget that Miguel d'Escoto and Ernesto Cardenal, two priests who became part of the government, had tried for a number of years to propose a nonviolent alternative to the popular forces and, above all, to the church, which had access to the people and enjoyed their confidence. Their voices were not heard in time, even though the most farsighted bishops had made explicit explorations in this direction a little before the conflict: thus the archbishop of Managua took part in a seminar on nonviolence, held at Bogotá in December 1977, with twenty bishops of the whole continent. There remain evident marks of this concern in the style of living out the conflict. The revolution in Nicaragua was one of the most humane recorded in history. There was a real effort, often heroic, to avoid shedding blood. After the victory the firing-squad was disbanded. There were stunning cases of pardon when yesterday's victims who found themselves face to face with the murderers who had wiped out their families renounced the thought of vengeance.

A revolution continues as it began: "One sows what one reaps" (Gal. 6:8). The Vietnamese revolution was militarized, and the nation continues along the same line. Likewise, each time that Christianity has used force to impose itself, history has taken its vengeance. Saint Augustine used force to bring the Donatists back in, and today the church of Africa no longer exists. We may think of Charlemagne with the Saxons; the Inquisition; the Wars of Religion of the Reformation epoch, which discredited Christianity and perhaps prepared the way for European atheism; the bloody evangelization of Latin America; the United States Civil War, when Christians reading the same Bible fought each other ferociously. This history of violence has left its mark on our collective behavior today.

Nicaragua had the good fortune to expel Somoza without an intervention from the United States. But the possibility of an armed intervention from North America was not eliminated: the contras have been covertly supplied with aid, an economic embargo has been imposed. Here the old law again applies: since the revolution was carried out by force of arms, despite the desire for nonviolence, likewise the resistance to intervention will be in the same manner. A genuinely nonviolent revolution requires more time for preparation (which was not available in Nicaragua); but it will last longer because it cannot be overthrown in the same way by the force of arms.

Perhaps what was lacking in Nicaragua was the availability of a clear option for the mystique and practice of nonviolence, and systematic training of communities for such an action. Perhaps it was the theologians more than the pastors who were to blame. Pastors frequently sense such problems, for they live near the people; but it is the business of thinkers to explain their intuition, develop it, to make it clear enough so that it can be passed on.

Each strategy is all of a piece. An armed, violent combat has advantages and disadvantages. The mystique of "Thou shalt not kill" leads to a specific and different technique of combat: to a different type of mass training, and to a special formation of their leaders.

Finally let us hear what Miguel d'Escoto, priest and minister of foreign affairs, said in an interview with the *Catholic Worker* at Managua in December 1978 — that is, before the uprising. He explained that the understanding of the cross had been so distorted in Latin America that there was no hope of making the seed of active nonviolence germinate there. The environment was lacking: traditionally, in Latin America, we are inclined to look at the cross as a lamentable object, which makes us weep, especially during Lent and Holy Week, as something that should not have happened, instead of contemplating it as the most magnificent act of *life* in existence. *Nonviolence should be considered as a constitutive element in the preaching of the gospel.* This comes down to saying that, in my opinion, we do not preach the gospel today as we should, as long as we do not spread the spirituality and the concept of nonviolence as a means of liberation from oppression. That is essential for evangelization. This is not a devotion left up to each one's free choice. The cross is not something we can take or leave. The cross is not optional. The cross is something central. We should preach the cross, and to preach the cross is to preach nonviolence. Not the nonviolence of submission, but the nonviolence that consists in risking our life for the sake of fraternity. When we do that, we suffer reprisals from those who oppress the others. That is the cross. When we take up the cross, we participate in the birth-pangs of the Christ who suffers violence so as to engender the new humanity.

THE THEOLOGICAL APPROACH

The considerations just reviewed are already theological and are leading us to the third point of view from which we may speak about nonviolence, the theological.

"Love Your Enemies" (Luke 6:27)

What does this saying of Jesus mean? Above all, it is realistic. It means in the first place we have enemies, including class enemies; conflict exists. But in the second place, it affirms also that these enemies are children of the same God "who makes the sun shine on the evil and good, and rains on the just and unjust" (Matt. 5:45). So the class struggle cannot be deprived of its ethical dimensions. More than that: the enemy, even a class enemy, must be allowed to "feel" this love and this respect, if we do not wish to empty Jesus' word of its content. In any case it cannot be claimed that we love our enemies while at the same time we are unfortunately obliged to kill them! So the question is this: How shall we carry out a "political" and indeed military translation of this commandment of the Lord? How shall we live out the struggle for justice so that it will be at once effective and evangelical? It is evident that our struggle is not neutral; with open eyes it chooses the side of the poor, and at the same time acquires a set of enemies. But this combat must take its inspiration from Jesus' way of conducting himself when he had to deal with his enemies. Jesus, it seems, absolutely rejected two means of combating his enemies: (1) the physical death of the adversary; (2) the contempt that spells the moral death of the adversary when one says to the person, "For me, it is as if you were dead."

Jesus spoke very forceful words, had angry moments, even times of violence, but he never carried out an attack on human life. Even psychologically, for him, his adversary remains "somebody"; the adversary continues to exist. That is the whole point. If God exists, God is the God of all. The words "companion" (one who shares the same bread) and "comrade" (one who shares the same room) are not sufficient by themselves; we must also add "brother" and "sister."

Clarifying an Ambiguity

To say that violence is not according to the gospel does not mean that it is always avoidable. Unfortunately not! But those who are constrained to kill should not say that they have killed out of love! They should say that the weight of evil has been so heavy on them and on the others, that they have been pushed into the corner of using a method that is not evangelical. And let us add this: neither morally nor politically can a nonviolent solution be improvised; if a whole historical process of struggle is traveling toward a violent outcome, a nonviolent outcome cannot suddenly be improvised. It is with nonviolence as with the incarnation of Jesus: it comes at the summit of a gradual ascent of human history marked out by the sacrifice of thousands of saints, known or unknown, through whom humanity has become used to grace. Space had to be created for the incarnation to be possible. Therefore only the appearance of a historical dynamic, at once mystical and political, can make struggles of active nonviolence possible; and that in turn presupposes hard work, an intense and organized militancy, to which the churches are even yet only sparingly dedicated.

The reality of scandal exists: "It is impossible that scandals should not come, but woe to that one by whom they come," Jesus warns us (Luke 17:1). The evil in the world and in us is so strong that even Christians engaged in living the gospel in a radical manner by their baptism do not always reach the point of living fully the law of love. And thus the order left us by Christ, "love even your enemies," is not obeyed and grace undergoes a serious setback, the kingdom recedes. The responsibility is collective and not solely (or primarily) the act of those who have been backed into violent situations. We can passively allow injustices to be heaped up to such a degree in some corner of the planet that brothers and sisters, even Christians, will be overwhelmed and in practice forced to take up arms. Look at what is going on in El Salvador, Guatemala, perhaps in Poland. The poor, the oppressed, who are thus in effect forced to take up arms, are much closer to the gospel attitude than many other Christians; for their violence, which resists injustice, certainly contains more love than the absence of violence in those who are merely passive in the face of evil. There are three classes: those "without violence," the lukewarm whom God will spew out (Rev. 3:16); the violent, who do something; and the authentic nonviolent, who struggle against evil with the arms of love. Gandhi said in effect: "If you cannot be nonviolent, at least be violent; what you must not be is indifferent, refraining from taking a position in the face of injustice."

When all that has been said, *we must not call evil "good."* Killing is an absolute evil for which we are responsible. This evil could have been avoided if we had worked harder at our individual purification and at the organization of great popular movements, which would then be animated by this spirit and able to withdraw popular support from an unjust social order. The idols stay on their thrones because we do not dare push them off by disobeying them. Active nonviolence will make no ethical concession to the existence of violence. Then we shall have to say that the least bad violence is still bad, and that *the theology of the just war is not a Christian theology.*

The Principal Axis of a Future Theology of Nonviolence

Around us we hear endless analyses of the texts of Scripture and of the practice of the saints to find a loophole for "Christian" violence: Jesus, who expels the moneychangers from the temple, who "kills" the fig tree, who advises his disciples to sell their cloak and buy a sword (Luke 22:36). (This last verse is a metaphorical saying of Jesus describing the universal hostility surrounding the disciples; at John 18:11 Jesus tells Peter to put his sword back in its sheath, and at Matt. 26:52 he foresees that those who take the sword will perish by the sword.) It is recalled that Saint Bernard preached the Crusades, that Joan of Arc expelled the English from France by force of arms in obedience to her voices, that warrior saints like Martin and George are not rare in Christianity.

It seems to us that our reflection should be differently centered, if we wish not to be lost in details and endless disputes of interpretation. In Christianity as everywhere else there is the subordinate and essential. What is the profound dynamic of the gospel? As for myself, I believe that this dynamic is nonviolent because the axis of the gospel is the resurrection. *It is from the resurrection of Jesus that a nonviolent theology is to be deduced.* Look at it this way.

Christ is risen: What does that mean for our daily lives? Most simply, this: that life is stronger than death, good greater than

evil, grace more powerful than *dis*grace. Then any struggle that
in its *methodology* includes death inflicted on another as a principle of action distances itself to that precise degree from the
axis of the kingdom. For how in fact can one still be included
in the sphere of the kingdom, which is life and resurrection, how
can one belong to this space of the kingdom that is defined by
the triumph of life over death, if one inflicts death on another?
The two are incompatible. Scripture says, "Without bloodshed
there is no forgiveness" (Heb. 9:22). The whole question is:
Whose blood? If it is the blood of one's enemy, one is no longer
identified with the Lamb of God that takes way the sins of the
world: one takes away the *life* of the adversary, not the sin; one
pulls up the good grain along with the tares. If it is one's own
blood, then everything changes, and one's sacrifice is proof that
one resisted injustice. The masses, as we said, are always moved
by the sacrifice of the just one, and they set themselves in turn
to reject infamous social structures. They pass from passive nonviolence to active nonviolence.

We have also explained that active nonviolence is not a suicidal attitude: before sacrificing one's life, one needs to learn
how to give it for a cause. Hence that intense militancy of which
I have spoken. Miguel d'Escoto, in the passage quoted, shows
that he has very deeply perceived what must be the authentic
methodology of the kingdom: a renewed sense of the cross.
Cross and resurrection are indissolubly linked. If we have been
snatched out of the empire of darkness to enter into the kingdom of God — that is, into that part of reality where death has
been eliminated — the only method of combat remaining to us is
the cross and not the revolver. We confront evil and accept in
our flesh the blows of the adversary, knowing that such an attitude moves profoundly, on the level of the best that is in them,
thousands of persons of goodwill. Only the hardened are un-
reachable; the sacrifice of the just one liberates the lukewarm
from their sins and isolates the evildoers. This is the way in
which the Lamb of God continues the redemptive mission today
in the person of disciples.

And what about the hardened? one will ask. Are they ex-
cluded? That is a mystery. We must not despair of the salvation,
the regeneration, of anybody. Not even of Hitler or Somoza.

What is sure, on the level of action, is that persons of this sort will not change except when forced and constrained by popular pressure. The question is: By what sort of popular pressure? We have explained here the kind that we are thinking of: the pressure of the humble, of the poor who, without magnifying themselves by using the weapons of the powerful, refuse to go on any longer obeying injustice, whatever the consequences, and hold up before the evil the shining face of a pure and humble love that does not blow out the smoking wick, but also does not lower its eyes, any more than Jesus did at his trial.

The resurrection, as the fundamental orienting principle of Christian behavior, can throw fresh light on all kinds of situations in which we or our societies live. How to behave in daily life? How should society be organized to deal with crime? Until the end of time, crimes and punishments will exist. There exist prisons, police commissioners, sentences. Is not prison a violence done to the human person, which the church accepts with a tranquil heart? And the death penalty? For centuries Christian theologians have not felt obliged to say anything in criticism of it. It seems to us that the criterion of the resurrection can help us to see more clearly. Every punishment that comes down to a purely repressive function, for example, by isolating a dangerous person, is on the order of death, and therefore unworthy of the kingdom. But if the punishment is conceived of in such a way that it can genuinely exercise the function of rehabilitation, it reenters the dynamic of the kingdom. Thus it is conceivable for a "nonviolent" criminal-justice system to exist: that is, a system designed to restore life to the one who has lost it. We know that some are taking steps in this direction.

CONCLUSION

Here, as a conclusion, are the "trump cards" of active nonviolence — its strategic advantages over against armed struggle — and the commandments of nonviolence.

The Trump Cards of Active Nonviolence in Brazil

1. The force of the poor is their number, which is always increasing.

2. The force of the poor comes also from the place that they occupy in the economy. They have their fingers on the levers of the machines and they handle the means of production.

3. The weakness of the poor is their disorganization and lack of unity. To unite the poor and organize them is where nonviolence has its most original proposition: it is the *purity* of their combat that most unites the humble. That is a truth ignored by a great number of those who struggle for justice. It is a moral phenomenon. The little ones can be united more durably and in greater numbers, with more firmness and courage, around the just one, persecuted and unarmed, than around a leader in war, even if that leader is reasonably humane and is conducting a "just" war. To achieve this unity requires that there be children of God, "good shepherds," who walk ahead to show the way and to render the combat public and organized.

The Commandments of Active Nonviolence in Brazil

1. Do not kill.
2. Never wound by word or deed.
3. Always be united, alert, and organized.
4. Start from local struggles and organize collective struggles.
5. Act with *unyielding firmness;* do not draw back.
6. Know how to risk your life; overcome the fear of death; do not run away.
7. Do not hide anything. [Nonviolence cannot be clandestine—it would deny itself, for all its strength comes from the truth.]
8. Stay clear of hatred; pray for your enemies.
9. Purify yourself constantly.
10. Disobey laws and orders that attempt to destroy the people and their organizations.

Chapter 11

Christ and Politics

> *"Return to Caesar what is Caesar's,*
> *and to God what is God's."*

The mistake so many Christians make in their political battle is partly due to a mistaken view of Jesus' own struggle.

His battle was first and foremost a religious one. As the Lord's anointed, he had come primarily to heal human beings of their diseased relationships. Practically all of humanity's joys and sorrows are due to the way human beings relate to God and to one another. The word "religion" probably means a binding (cf. "ligament"). Religion is a relationship.

What we call grace is a marvelous, supernatural happening, an event beyond the powers of our nature. Grace is the coming of a new reign, the unexpected event of a wholesome, creative relationship between two or more persons.

But when we say that Jesus' combat was "religious," we do not mean that politics is missing from the gospel. On the contrary, politics is one of the most important relationships a human person can maintain. The political aspect does not exhaust human relationships, which are infinitely rich (their font and origin being God) and cover many fields of activity maintained by this mysterious phenomenon known as the human being. But no one,

This essay originally appeared in Portuguese in *A Firmeza-Permanente* by Antônio Fragoso, et al. (São Paulo, 1977). The translation is by Robert R. Barr.

not even a Christian who tends to be very backward in this area, can deny that the political is a basic dimension of the human.

THE POLITICAL DIMENSION OF FAITH

A Concrete Example — Public Transportation

Let me begin with a concrete example. Recently our church region decided to launch a campaign to have a bus as our form of participation in the annual Lenten Fellowship Campaign. The archbishop of São Paulo himself had encouraged the archdiocese to give some attention to the bothersome problem of transportation. The idea was to share our bread and to share a difficulty touching our whole population.

Why did the base communities of our church region respond with such little enthusiasm? Of three urban sectors, with forty to fifty communities, only some fifteen showed any interest in the bus project. And of these, most failed to appear when the time came to act.

The bus campaign could have had a certain degree of success if all or nearly all the communities had joined forces.

Why this attitude? Fear? Lack of time? (But we have time for baptisms, premarital courses, retreats, and other church activities.) The difficulty of "conscientizing" the people — raising consciousness, making them aware of their needs? Perhaps a bit of all three. But there is another obstacle too, one that we might call ideological. In this case, it is theological. It might be formulated as follows. Since when is a campaign for the improvement of public transportation a task of evangelization? Since when is it the church's business to get involved in municipal administration? Since when is it our responsibility to question the monopoly of the big bus companies?

We answered these valid questions at the outset of the campaign, in simple terms everyone could understand. When you take a bus, you are no longer in the kingdom of God. Public transportation is that bad. It is up to us Christians, then, whose mission it is to further the growth of the reign of God, to improve public transportation. In other words, a campaign for the improvement of transportation is a *religious* task. It *links* human beings with the living God, who is peace and harmony. And we recalled the theology of the last synod, which proclaimed to the bishops of the entire world:

> Christian salvation is struggle with the powers of sin and death (Col. 1:16). These powers manifest their presence today by way of pestilence, starvation, war, oppression, torture, exploitation, slavery, eroticism, inadequate wages, and so on. Men and women expect concrete deeds from the Christian church in behalf of the greater part of humanity, so marginalized and oppressed by these powers of death [Intervention of Bishop Paulo in the Synod, October 9, 1974].

Was fighting for the improvement of transportation not a "concrete deed"? Then why such massive indifference? Apart from the schools, the shelter campaign, and educational assistance, when does our local church ever serve the people with "concrete deeds"? True, any concern with transportation is, indirectly, politics. When you have to do with a public entity that serves a whole population, like it or not you get involved in politics. We are not suggesting that the church as such should take on a "professional" political function. We only mean that, in as much as politics is the art of living in society, when you try to influence the social life of a municipality in any way you are practicing politics in the broad sense of the word.

As we know, even someone who refuses to "get mixed up in this sort of thing," is also practicing politics by virtue of the very refusal. An attitude of neutrality is itself a political choice, and has political consequences. Indirectly, but really, it is a choice in favor of the powers that be, for it is a choice for leaving them to do just as they please. It is a decision betraying a basic unconcern with the common good.

Not that we look down on the reserved attitude of our Catholic base communities. The question of the relationship between faith and politics is a delicate one, and it occupies the best theological minds of Latin America. Does Christian salvation include a political liberation? How? To what extent? What is salvation anyway?

In the following pages I should like to formulate some theoretical principles that might help us improve the quality of our activity in current circumstances. We want to make our action more effective. Theology is more than just a speculative science. It must lead to action. "Not those alone who say, 'Lord, Lord' . . ."! Theology is the tireless attempt to apply Jesus' message to the movements of history—in order to place the yeast of the gospel at the deepest heart of the earth.

THE CHURCH AND POLITICS

History

Were we to add up the hours the church has spent supporting the established order, and weigh them against the seconds it has spent opposing it, we should surely find that the hours outnumber the seconds. Nikolai Berdyaev felt constrained to say that "Christianity has been deformed by its adaptation to the reign of Caesar. The church has bowed to the power of the state, and has sought to sacralize that power." This is no exaggeration. We need only read the history of the last century and a half, for example, to see to what point, and with what rare constancy, the church has taken sides with every counterrevolution. It did not even oppose, forthrightly and with all its strength, the Nazi abomination! In 1877, after the Paris Commune had slaughtered thousands of the working class (over 20,000 in a week, with 43,000 confined as political prisoners), Corbon, once a laborer and now a senator, confided to Dupanloup, one of the most illustrious of the Frence bishops of that time:

> *Monseigneur,* we abondon you today because you abandoned us *centuries ago.* When I say you abandoned us, I do not mean you refused us the comforts of religion. Your own priestly interest dictated you lavish those on us. *What I mean is that for centuries you have left our temporal cause in the lurch, and have exerted your influence to impede rather than to further our temporal redemption.*[1]

Again, who does not recall that the publication of the Communist Manifesto (1848) antedated *Rerum Novarum* (1891) by a half-century? It took the Catholic Church fifty years after Marx to wake up to the traumatic condition of the working classes! How could the church have been unaware of the fact that children of eight and eleven were working 10 to 14 hours a day in the sweatshops of England, France, and Germany at the beginning of the last century?

With the Industrial Revolution, the factory became the place most hated and feared by adults. For children it was even worse. The owners wanted one thing only—the cheapest possible manpower. Children, frequently thrust into the world of machines from five years old onward, received no wages, only food and a place to sleep. They were treated like little prisoners, and were forbidden to leave the factory grounds. They were chained like puppies, not only to punish them when they had disobeyed, but simply to keep them at their machines, lest they creep off to a corner and go to sleep. The factories of Lancashire, the mines of Wales, were full of these little unfortunates. Most of them came from the so-called workhouses. Exactly as in the case of Oliver Twist, the owners of the industries "bought" the children from the authorities, who were overjoyed to be rid of them. Children were simply bought and sold, as they had been in the days of slavery. They awakened hungry and went to sleep with empty stomachs. They did not know the meaning of play. They knew only the fear of the whip. Divided into groups of fifty or a hundred, they had to live at least seven years in the factories to which they had been sold. At the end of that time they emerged physically, emotionally, and morally destroyed. At times the authorities saw to it that the mentally handicapped were included in this horrible traffic. Suicide was common among factory children. "Their life," as someone once put it, "is a perfect image of hell."[2]

Suppose Christians were still to have an attitude like this, for example, vis-à-vis the Third World. Would this not cast serious doubt on the very meaning of Christianity in the world today? Christian, where is your "good news"? Do you have anything good to say to us for this world we live in? Thousands of human beings, with whom we mingle every day, address us this mute question.

Jean and Hildegard Goss-Mayr, pioneers in many nonviolent campaigns around the world, heard the following shocking words from a priest working in Angola: "The trauma of Angolan Christians and their church is such that the church is totally useless here." And the Goss-Mayrs comment:

> This is a hard saying. It means that the "white church" has failed to get its message of the liberation of the poor, which is the be-all and end-all of the gospel itself, through to the people. It means that the church has the strength to transform neither the history of oppressed Africans nor the white servants of colonialism. We have to have the courage to look at this wound, and see how deep it is, if we are to manage a radical change. How else can we create within ourselves a humility that will win forgiveness, that we may begin really to live the gospel of Christ among the people?

If we wish to change from dough into yeast, we must probably recognize that the Christian church in China, the Soviet Union, Europe, and yes, Latin America, is far more willing to live in peace with Caesar than oppose him when need be. Perhaps this "accommodationism" partly explains why Christianity has lost its radiant force. We offer sacrifices to the idols of the empire. It is a well-known fact that moral theologians regard the duty of obedience to the state a "grave obligation in conscience." They base their conclusion on certain passages in the New Testament. But let us examine some of these texts, and see whether their conclusion is really justified.

Scripture

The Gospel according to Saint Matthew

"Restore to Caesar what is Caesar's and to God what is God's" (Matt. 22:21). Jesus is giving a very specific answer to an extremely circumstantial question here. Yet his words have been used to base a whole ecclesial practice of unconditional obedience to the state. The objective of Jesus' reply is not to develop an entire political theology, but to avoid falling into a trap. The Pharisees think they have Jesus on the horns of a dilemma. If they can lure him into taking a position on taxation, they reason, either they will deprive him of his authority with the people, because he has recommended paying taxes to the hated Romans, or else they will be able to denounce him to the Roman authorities for advising precisely that the taxes not be paid. But Jesus will not take the bait. He specifically commands his audience only to return to Caesar what is Caesar's. It is not a matter of a contribution, but of a repayment. And his response culminates in the resounding "Return to God what is God's"! Jesus is simply applying the classic principle of Jewish casuistry: the chosen people of God must never forget that it has a messianic mission to "give glory to God amid the gentiles."

Why have theologians not retained this basic content? Why have they forgotten that Jesus is saying that everything belongs to God? Saint Paul never forgot. "All things are yours," he cried, "and you are Christ's and Christ is God's." In the case at hand: because the political area belongs to God, we should give glory to God by our manner of living in society. Jesus taught that the obedience due God was the most important thing in the world, just as the law of Moses had long ago proclaimed: "You shall love your God, and serve him alone" (Deut. 6:13). Jesus would not put God and the state on an equal footing. The state may not be worshipped. The first Christians were persecuted because they refused to offer sacrifice to Caesar, and refused to cry out, *"Kyrios Caesar,* Caesar is Lord!" We may scarcely conclude from Jesus' reply to the Pharisees that we have a duty to obey Caesar in all circumstances!

The teaching of the church on obedience to the state is quite complex and nuanced. And it has undergone modification in the course of the centuries. When the civil order—the order of Caesar—places obstacles in the way of "the growth of the reign of God and God's justice" (Matt. 6:33), that order is to be disobeyed. God is the only absolute, the only legitimate object of worship and adoration. Saint Peter knew this too well to submit even to the legitimate authorities of his people when they prescribed a transgression of the law of God: "It is better to obey

God than men," he said (Acts 5:29), and his saying has been a
thorn in the side of the powers of Christendom all down the
centuries. In fact, "hearing these words, the members of the
Council [the Sanhedrin] were beside themselves with rage, and
resolved to slay the Apostles" (Acts 5:33). Disobedience to unjust laws, be they economic, political, or religious laws, is a duty
in conscience, for "law is for the sake of humankind, and not
humankind for the sake of law," as Jesus declares in a familiar
passage—to which Christians would do very well to attend when
defining their political attitude (Matt. 2:23–38).

Indeed, this text, which shows us that Jesus allowed his disciples to disobey a perverted religious law, defines the way we
ought to live in society. We may not hold law in contempt, but
neither may we absolutize it. To absolutize it would be idolatry.
It is not laws that delimit right and justice, but right and justice
that must summon forth the existence of laws. Law ought to
contain a "self-destruct" mechanism, so that when it trampled
right and justice under foot it would blow itself sky-high. The
prophet Isaiah cried: "Woe to those who make unjust laws, and
to judges who pronounce oppressive sentences, who refuse to
do justice to the poor, and who violate the rights of the little
ones of my people, who abuse widows and plunder orphans"
(Isa. 10:1ff.). Disobedience to the state can be a duty of conscience, then.

The church must not teach Christians simply to obey the law.
It should teach them to judge the law. Then, when they have
passed their Christian judgment on it, they ought to be prepared
to abide by it as a matter of conscience if it serves justice, but
equally ready to disobey it if it no longer really does so. Jesus
himself pointedly warns his disciples that fidelity to his word
means risking conflict with the authorities: "For my sake they
will be hailed before kings, to testify before them and the gentiles" (Matt. 10:18). The princes of this world do not suffer
prophets gladly. And the only way they have ever found to silence them is to kill them.

But you can only stifle an individual voice. You cannot stifle
the voice of truth.

Jesus' trial fairly rings with irony here. No one managed to
gather the truth gushed from the cross. Christ was brought down

to death by those who hated the Roman Caesar and yet who had sold themselves to him to silence a voice that it hurt them to have to listen to. "Shall I crucify your king?" Pilate asked the rabble (John 19:15). "Render to Caesar what is Caesar's," wrote Saint John Chrysostom, "means give Caesar what you can without ceasing to serve God. For to give to Caesar what is God's would be to pay a tax not to Caesar, but to Satan."

LETTER TO THE ROMANS

A follower of Jesus has the right and duty to subject the state to a critical appraisal, in light of the absolute criterion of the reign of God as proclaimed in the gospels. When the state seeks to apply the rule of justice, it should be obeyed, and "not only out of fear of punishment, but simply in order to obey the voice of conscience" (Rom. 13:5). After all:

All authority is from God. There is no authority that does not come from God, and the powers that be were instituted by him. Thus he who resists authority rebels against the order established by God [Rom. 13:1–2].

Few passages in the New Testament have been misused as much as this one has. Let someone so much as accuse the state of overstepping its bounds, and the constituted authorities or their theological advisers will at once appeal to this saying of the Apostle, as if Paul had intended to make it our Christian duty to approve the politics of our country and even to take part in its crimes. Many who decided to obey Hitler and his butchers and help exterminate Jews during the Second World War were Christians. Why in the world should Christians think they are conscience-bound to do such a thing? Why should Christians have to fight a war they think unjust? Why must they side with their country's nuclear policy? If the passage under consideration were intended to establish absolute, unconditional obedience as the Christian rule, Saint Paul would be contradicting Jesus, the rest of the New Testament, especially the Book of Revelation, and even himself! Saint Paul would never have allowed the Christians of his churches to give to Caesar what is God's—to cry, "*Kyrios Caesar,* Caesar is Lord," or say "*Anath-*

ema Jesus, Jesus be damned," as some Christians actually did some years after Paul's death, in the age of the great persecution.

When the state steps out of its function "to be an instrument of God"—an instrument only, not an idol—"to lead persons to do good" (Rom. 13:4), it loses its authority to bind consciences.

Futhermore, this text of the Apostle on obedience to authority has received various interpretations. Gregory XVI, in his *Mirari Vos,* wrote:

> Let all attentively consider that, in conformity with the Apostle's warning, there is no power that does not come from God. ... To resist authority is to resist the order established by God. ... Human and divine law rise up in accusation against men who, by blackest maneuver of revolt and sedition, strive to destroy the fidelity due to princes and topple them from their thrones.

But the Second Vatican Council modifies this interpretation considerably:

> It is therefore obvious that the political community and public authority are based on human nature and hence belong to an *order of things divinely foreordained.* At the same time the choice of government and the method of selecting leaders is left to the free will of citizens [*Gaudium et Spes,* no. 74, emphasis added].

Let us observe that the conciliar text no longer speaks of the political community and public authority as belonging to a "divine order" that human beings must obey. Now they speak of a divinely foreordained order—an intention in the mind of God *as to* the organization of a society. This is quite a different matter.

THE BOOK OF REVELATION

Other New Testament texts make it possible to complete our definition of the authentic Christian attitude toward the state. The texts we have in mind are to be found in the last book of the Bible, the Book of Revelation. Revelation was written in a climate of persecution, at a time when the state had begun persecuting Christians. Practically the whole of Saint Paul's mission, on the other hand, had been exercised in the absence of any systematic hostility on the part of the Romans. In the early decades, Christianity did not yet represent a serious danger to public order. The difference in historical situation is interesting, for it occasions the appearance of texts, equally inspired by the Spirit, which balance those of the letters of Saint Paul:

> Revelation was written either after the persecution of Nero (A.D. 65–70), or, more probably, at the close of the reign of Domitian (A.D. 71–96). Domitian sought to promote emperor-worship, which would explain Revelation's concern to demonstrate the irreducible opposition between the reign of the Lord Jesus and the blasphemous reign of Caesar [*Bible Oecuménique*].

When the state oversteps its function and absolutizes itself, it is no longer an instrument of God for the accomplishment of justice and for leading men and women to the good. It has become an instrument of Satan. Now, far from taking any account of God's justice, Satan is extremely interested in having human beings fall into the temptation to idolatry. Many persons, indeed, driven by the powerful machinations of the state (propaganda, power, prestige, and so on) refuse to be converted to the worship of God, and absolutize "works made by human hands"—the gross national product, the glory of the fatherland, technology, and so on. They deny the sovereignty of the Lord Jesus, and cry out with the enemies of the Lamb: "We have no king but Caesar. To him be the power, the glory, and the praise, for he promises us safety, comfort, wealth, and grandeur."

Then there rises up out of the abyss (the sea) the monster of which the Book of Revelation tells. That beast, whose numerology is that of "a certain man" (Rev. 13:18), has always represented, in Christian tradition, Caesar—political power at the service of evil. The sacred writer explains that the dragon, who is Satan, "gave it his own power and throne, together with great authority" (Rev. 13:2). And the beast "began to hurl blasphemies against God, reviling him and the members of his heavenly household as well" (Rev. 13:6). Then another monster appears, this time from out of the earth. The second monster represents false prophets (Rev. 16:13; 19:20; 20:10). This second beast is at the service of the first, and constrains all the dwellers of earth to worship the image of the beast (Rev. 13:15).

This beast—representing false prophets—works great wonders, and succeeds in seducing many:

> It forced all men, small and great, rich and poor, slave and free, to accept a stamped image on their right hand or their forehead. Moreover, it did not allow a man to *buy or sell* anything unless he was first marked with the name of the beast or with the number that stood for its name [Rev. 13:16–17].

It is important to note that *the work of the monster requires control of the power of gain*. But "if anyone worships the beast or its image, or accepts its mark on his forehead or hand, he too will drink the wine of God's wrath, poured full strength into the cup of his anger. . . . There shall be no relief day or night" (Rev. 14:10). For they have been willing to offer sacrifice to the pagan idols of Babylon the Great, the realm of great Caesar (Rev. 18), and have forgotten the law of justice and love.[3] And yet it had been engraved on their hearts! The disciples of the Lamb, who have never abandoned God's justice to go and serve Caesar, shall have their names written in the Book of Life. They shall escape condemnation, for "on their lips no deceit has been found; they are indeed without flaw" (Rev. 14:5). Here we have a radical condemnation of lying in the service of power and authority. Whenever Caesar betrays the truth, enticing men and women to worship false values that are not directed to the glory of God, we have an obligation in conscience to disobey this human law, humbly but openly, even at the risk of being punished for doing so.

MATTHEW 4:7–10

> The devil then took him up a very high mountain and displayed before him all the kingdoms of the world in their

magnificence, promising, "All these will I bestow on you if you prostrate yourself in homage before me." At this, Jesus said to him, "Away with you, Satan! Scripture has it: 'You shall do homage to the Lord your God; him alone shall you adore.'"

JOHN 6:14–15

When the people saw the sign he had performed they began to say, "This is undoubtedly the Prophet who is to come into the world." At that, Jesus realized that they would come and carry him off to make him king, so he fled back to the mountain alone.

All the texts on which I have commented up to this point bear on a central biblical theme — a theme as old as the Bible itself: one may not make anyone, even Caesar, into an idol. The root of all evil was identified by the prophets as the sin of idolatry. Obedience to the state must end the moment that the state encourages us to abandon the adoration of the one, true God and to go running after "other gods." We have no sovereign but Jesus Christ.

Both of the texts presented here seem to show us a Jesus steadfastly refusing all political power. After all, he is repelling the temptation of sovereignty. Consequently, some theologians say, Christians may not place Christianity at the service of any political liberation, for they would thereby be ignoring the word of God and succumbing to the diabolical temptation that Christ so pointedly exposed and overcame (Matt. 4:7–10). The salvation brought by Christ is of another kind, we are told. Jesus judged the political institution to be altogether too ambiguous to use to incarnate his liberating activity. A Christian's political activity can be a good thing. Christians may and should take part in the construction of this world. But the church as such must not assume political commitments. It has another mission.

This position is incomplete, and thereby misleading. It will incline Christians and their church to adopt an attitude of partiality toward the established order. It will encourage Christians to maintain a reactionary, or at least a conservative, attitude in the area of politics. Because Christ's sovereignty does not include the area of the political, we are told, then obviously it must endorse the established social order so long as that order does not prejudice the interests of the church or the essential points of faith and Christian morality (including concordats — treaties between the Vatican and the various states).

This attitude is not without a latent hypocrisy. Political neutrality, as I remarked in the beginning of this chapter, is itself a political choice. Witness the fact that, over the centuries, the church tolerated and even blessed regimes that refused to respect the most elementary human rights. And it continues to do so today:

> Thus, the state can judge, condemn, humiliate, imprison, and ultimately deliver to death a multitude of men and women, with the indulgent complicity of a church that has resigned itself to such "necessities" in view of the "historical situation of the moment."[4]

My interpretation of these texts is different. The thesis I criticize is based on the *fundamental idea* that Jesus refused political sovereignty as a temptation of the devil. To my view, Jesus' thinking is more complex than this. Indeed, from another point of view we might even say just the opposite: Jesus never refused sovereignty, not even over this world. He only rejected the idolatrous manner in which human beings seek to exercise power (Caesar, for example) or come to power (the Zealots, for example, the major guerrilla movement of Jesus' time and place).

Hence this capital consequence: the church as such must take an attitude that includes political liberation. It may not maintain neutrality vis-à-vis Caesar, even if this will cost it a great deal of persecution, indeed the provisional destruction of its temporal organism. Let me explain why I hold this to be true.

THE KINGDOM OF GOD

Countless New Testament passages proclaim the coming of a mysterious reign destined to transform the shape of this world from top to bottom. The kingdom or reign of God, an expression that occurs 122 times in the Gospels, 90 of these on the lips of Christ, represents a total, structural revolution in the foundations of this world, to be introduced by God. Christ "began to preach the kingdom of God." What does the kingdom of God, so clearly the center of his message, stand for? For Jesus' audience it meant something very different from what it means to the ears of the modern believer, for whom it is merely the next life, heaven, life after death. For Jesus' hearers the kingdom of God meant the realization, at the end of the ages, of their hope of victory over all human alienations. It meant the destruction of all evil, physical and moral, the destruction of sin, hatred, division, sickness, and death. The kingdom of God was thought of as the manifestation of God's sovereign lordship over a disastrous world now dominated by satanic powers locked in mortal combat with the forces of good. It meant: God is the solitary meaning of this world. God will presently intervene to heal the whole of creation at its very root, establishing a new sky and a new earth. It is this hope, this desire of every nation, that is the object of Jesus' preaching. Jesus promises: this is no longer to be sheer hope. This will be reality. For God will cause it to be. Jesus preached this for the first time in the synagogue in Galilee, after having read a passage from Isaiah (66:1ff.):

> The Spirit of the Lord is upon me:
> wherefore he has anointed me.
> He has sent me to bring glad tidings to the poor,
> to proclaim liberty to captives,
> Recovery of sight to the blind,
> and release to prisoners,
> To announce a year of favor from the Lord
> [Luke 4:18–19].

Then he said: "Today this scripture passage is fulfilled in your hearing" (Luke 4:21).

To John the Baptist's question from prison: "Are you the one who is to come, or should we look for another?" Jesus responds: "The blind see, the lame walk, lepers are healed, the deaf hear, the dead rise, and the poor have the gospel preached to them" (Matt. 11:3–5). In other words, Jesus has brought about a complete turnaround. Now, the one who manages to introduce this sort of thing is the long-awaited liberator of the human race. For in the reign of God, illness, blindness, hunger, natural catastrophes, sin and death, will no longer occur.[5]

"This reign is in our midst" (Luke 17:21). "It has come to us" (Luke 14:20). Like yeast, it will be working in the dough that is humanity. Indeed, it has already begun to do so (Matt. 13:33). It begins humbly, like a mustard seed, but one day it will be a bush as big as a tree (Matt. 13:31). It comes not by the power of human beings and their weapons, but by the power of the word (Mark 4:26). In it good and evil are mixed (Matt. 13:24). As Saint Augustine said long ago, " 'my Reign is not of this world' (John 18:36), but it begins in this world."

Despite having manifested such great mistrust of the title of king (John 6:15), at least twice Jesus accepts it, with its political connotations. When he enters Jerusalem in triumph, before his passion, "the crowds following him cried out: 'Hosanna to the Son of David! Blessed is he who comes in the name of the Lord!' " (Matt. 21:5).

Even more clearly, arraigned before Pilate, Jesus refuses to deny the royal character of his mission:

"Pilate said to him, "So, then, you are a king?" Jesus replied: "It is you who say I am a king. The reason I was born, the reason why I came into the world, is to testify to the truth. Anyone committed to the truth hears my voice [John 18:37].

Jesus' enemies were right to see political implications in his preaching. "We found this man subverting our nation, opposing the payment of taxes to Caesar, and calling himself the Messiah, a king" (Luke 23:2).

One day the Jewish community of Thessalonica would fabricate the same reason to stir up the people against Paul and Silas:

These men have been creating a disturbance all over the place. Now they come here and Jason has taken them in.

To a man, they disregard the emperor's decrees and claim instead that a certain Jesus is king [Acts 17:6–7].

These excerpts should suffice to show that Jesus and the first Christians acted in such a way that the political consequences of the preaching of the reign became evident to all, Christians and pagans alike. Furthermore, it is our Christian hope that the kingship of Christ will finally extend to all aspects of social and political life. We can take literally this text from the Book of Revelation describing the final state of the reign:

Now have salvation and power come,
>   the reign of our God and the authority of his Anointed One.
For the accuser of our brothers is cast out,
>   who night and day accused them before our God
>   [Rev. 12:10].

The eschatological combat — the battle to be waged in the last days of creation, and which has already begun — is to be of a frankly political tenor. Those who wage the eschatological combat will necessarily be, and already are, in a political battle, for they fight for the new world that is the goal of Christian hope. They have handed down their judgment on political power. It is written that the hour is coming when the kings of the earth will hide in caves and mountain crags for fear of the wrath of the Lamb that was slain (Rev. 6:15–16). When Jesus says, "My kingdom does not belong to this world," he does not mean that his reign cannot grow in this world, on this earth, in our human society. Were this the case, we should certainly have the obligation to "flee the world," as a certain religious vocabulary puts it. On the contrary, in another passage Jesus explains that we must remain in this world, in order to do battle here: "Father, I do not ask you to take them out of the world, but to guard them from the evil one" (John 17:15). As we know, the word "world," in the language of Saint John, means the selfish world, the world under the domination of the powers of evil and sin.

THE NONVIOLENCE OF JESUS

But if Jesus did not refuse sovereignty over the world, why did he flee when his followers sought to proclaim him king? In my opinion, he did so only because he rejected the idolatrous form that this sovereignty would have to take in the circumstances. Satan had shown him "all the kingdoms of the world in their magnificence, promising, 'All these will I bestow on you if you prostrate yourself in homage before me.' At this Jesus said to him, 'Away with you, Satan! Scripture has it: You shall do homage to the Lord your God; him alone shall you adore' " (Matt. 4:8–10). This dialogue between Jesus and the Evil One is the condemnation of every temptation to false authority. Authority is false when it seeks to gain control over men and women by the seduction of glory and comfort or by the might of prestige, rather than by inviting them to surrender to a love that is freely offered.

Idolatry always aims to *violate human freedom*. It sparkles, it seduces, it compels. An idol is attractive, visible. The God proclaimed by Jesus is concealed. Jesus' God never seduces or forces. Ultimately the element of disease in human relationships supervenes when human relating ceases to be in the likeness of God. But God *never forces anyone*. In fact, God makes the sun of love to shine on good and wicked alike. (God's reward? Criticism and disbelief! See the parable of the prodigal, Luke 15:11–32.) When imposed by force, human relations become distorted. This perversion generates a hell of unbearable tensions, which thereupon explode in a collective violence that no one can control. Jesus knew this well, and warned his church of it. Immediately after proclaiming Peter's special role in the church, he has to admonish him severely. The prince of the apostles had sought to turn Jesus aside from the meekness and humility of his messianic kingship, a sovereignty of passion and death. The foundation stone of the church—Peter and Rome—will always be tempted by the prestige of power and glory—by idolatry, really. So will the bishops and their collaborators. And Jesus will always reprehend them, as he reprehended Peter on that day: "Get out of my sight, you satan! You are trying to make me trip and fall. You are not judging by God's standards but by human standards" (Matt. 16:23).

If God imposes on us not by force, but by love, then we too ought to impose ourselves not by force, but by active nonviolence. If it is really the living God who gives meaning to history, then each time we have recourse to violence and the lie for the purpose of establishing order and making progress, we delay the coming of the Lord. In fact, we delay the social revolution itself, for we are withdrawing society from an association with the sovereign of history itself. Jesus reserves his strongest protest for the idolatrous manner in which human beings relate to God and to one another. As we see, all idolatry leads to the violation of freedom. It pushes, it shoves, it forces. It uses violence, lying, and the seduction of vainglory. In the hands of an idol, the human being is bestialized, and becomes like the monster of the Book of Revelation who blasphemed God and God's chosen ones day and night. But this does not mean that Christ and his subjects must not win power over the world. On the contrary, that is exactly what they must do. Only, their weapons are now those of the Lamb of God who takes away the sins of the world.

Christ's exercise of royal power over the world will set the old order of things completely on its ear. That order had been adapted to a creation without grace or redemption. Now nonviolence becomes a possibility. "With the reign of Christ, a situation of nonviolence springs into being, not only individual, but social" (José Comblin). With the coming of the grace of redemption, "resources" appear in history by which the meek can come to possess the earth. The poor, those persecuted for justice' sake, the merciful, peacemakers, the pure of heart, now have a voice. They have been constituted heirs of the reign. The wealthy, the powerful, the violent are toppled from their thrones and sent empty away. Henceforth they have lost their power— *on condition that* there be champions of truth ready to confront them—without hatred and without fear.

With the coming of the grace of redemption, the world is now the scene of the sign of Jonah. As Jonah was three days in the belly of the great fish, so Christ was three days in the heart of the earth. There is an escape, a liberation, a resurrection! The sign of Jonah is always given by someone unarmed. The use of the weapons of this world, even for purposes of good, divests that sign of its effectiveness. When this happens, the wonders of death-and-resurrection, whether in the individual order or the social, cannot get started again.

Not everyone always has the opportunity of applying the gospel to life in all of its evangelical fullness. Inevitably, violent circumstances may arise at times, the fruit of humanity's collective sin. The human condition is tragic. It never ceases to strike at the fragile, divine edifice of the Beatitudes. But this is a scandal. And Jesus warns us that, while "it is inevitable that scandal should occur"—that violence should occur—"nonetheless, woe to that one through whom scandal comes!" (Matt. 18:7). Jesus knew how to avoid being this scandal—this stumbling block to the little ones of the reign who believe in the power of truth and the might of the Spirit. Jesus repelled temptations, even the most violent, and went straight to martyrdom rather than inaugurate his reign, even in the political and social area, by shedding the blood of others. We must carry on his work.

Let us understand well, then, the role of religion in the world. Religion is not directly a political task. It does, however, perform a genuinely subversive function. It prevents false orders of things from institutionalizing themselves. Jesus' protest against "this world," then, and the salvation he offers, are not primarily political, but *religious*, as stated at the beginning of this chapter. What do I mean by this?

The human being has a religious dimension. This is a fact of the very first importance. Religion means worship. But if we are deceived, we can worship something undeserving of our worship. Religion, like any other human instinct, is an ambiguous force, which can paralyze us or set us free. It can be alienating, or it can be precisely the opposite: liberating.

False religion, "closed" religion, is actually counterrevolutionary. It generates idolatry. It transports the Absolute to earth, in order to lead human beings to a *worship of limited, relative things*, which are not sacred, and which ought to change: for example, our country, our government, the organization of our church. When you begin to worship something, even something good, but limited, you no longer have the courage to touch it.

You are immobilized, paralyzed, in the contemplation of this idol. So it was that the Pharisees had come to worship the law of Moses, and refused to listen to Jesus' revolutionary explanation of the idolatrous nature of such worship. When you worship something good, but limited, you become ready to kill in order to defend the paltry reality you are willing to renounce. So it is that idolatrous Christians have tortured and killed their fellow Christians, and still torture and kill them, in the defense of "Christian civilization." The Soviets were another example of what the religious instinct can become when it deviated from its purpose. They paralyzed history, preserved the Soviet order, and killed twenty million Soviet citizens.

True religion—*open religion*—prevents men and women from making a definitive commitment to a limited thing, even a limited good thing. When all is said and done, *genuinely religious persons revere nothing*. They worship nothing. Why? Because they know that the Absolute they adore is not bounded by the confines of this world. We have a *dialectical* tension here—an oscillation between the existing world and the promised world, pushing forward to a definitive synthesis. The Absolute has a great deal at stake in this world. It has sunk deep roots here. But it also transcends this world, and seeks to draw it beyond current history—far beyond it. As a consequence, religious persons can worship nothing on the face of this earth, not even a new, revolutionary political order, however vital and authentic it might be. The function of authentic religion is critical: it prevents the idolatry that paralyzes history. All atheism runs the risk of absolutizing the relative and thereby stagnating the progress of history. Without the counterweight of an *open* religious dimension, any political movement can end by worshiping itself, thus causing its own death by suffocation (frequently in blood and tears).

Christianity may well be the only formal religion to have taught its devotees to use the religious impulse without falling into idolatry or abdicating their freedom.[6] The God proclaimed by Jesus:

1. Is infinite. God is always much more than we are able to conceive or imagine (see Eph. 3:20). We may never rest content with any image we have of God. In the same way, the new world,

which Jesus calls the reign of God, and which we must begin to create along with him, here and now, on this earth, will always transcend what we can accomplish.

2. Is adorable, but does not exact adoration. As we have said, God does not sparkle, God does not seduce, God does not use force. (We need only reread the account of the temptation of Christ, Matt. 4:11). God is a hidden Absolute, with whom we enter into contact *if we wish to*. One may very easily decide not to know God. The God of Jesus does not force our love. Why? Because God loves, and love cannot exact a return of love. We are not denying God's omnipotence. This love, this absolute love, is indeed omnipotent—*if we open the door to it*. This God, who is infinite but who respects our freedom, sets us free, and constantly opens us to the future. Here we have open religion. In a phase of acute social revolution, the role of open religion is not to develop programs, strategies, and tactics, but to enter into the revolutionary movement, with all the risks this will entail, in such a way as to keep that movement open to the future—committed to present history, yes, but turned toward the only Absolute, as well, lest revolutionaries themselves fall into an idolatry that paralyzes history—an idolatry of the revolution itself, however magnificent a thing that revolution might be.

Surely it is now clear why I disagree with the thesis that salvation in Christ does not include a political revolution, or that the church as such must not adopt a political attitude. When we take the gospel seriously, we see that it cannot tolerate collective situations that exclude the new world inaugurated by the Beatitudes. Jesus' battle with this world was nonviolent, yes. But it was radical. Jesus pulled evil up by the roots. He established a healthy, *wholesome* relationship—he established a religion—between human beings on the one hand, and God and creation on the other. This is why I say that the most drastic protest of the established order will always be religious. But I must add at once that religion involves and permeates the political. Gandhi came to see this.

If we would gaze upon the Spirit of Truth face to face,
in its universality,

in its capacity to penetrate all things,
we must acquire the ability to love —
to love ourselves,
and all creatures beside.

Once our hearts are fixed on this,
we can no longer rest content with a fixed idea
of this Spirit's exclusion
from any place whatsoever where life is manifested.
This is why my devotion to truth
led me to the area of the political.

And I can say without the least hesitation
that they understand nothing of religion
who deny that religion has anything to do with politics.[7]

Chapter 12

Transforming Love: An Interview with Dominique Barbé

How do you define nonviolence?

It's a form of combativeness that's very original and very powerful. Nonviolence is not just individual, it has a social and political character. It has a revolutionary aspect in that its end is to transform society. It aspires to a psychological as well as a religious attitude that makes conflict possible without bloodshed. The two necessary conditions of nonviolence are a deep moral-mystical purity and a high level of political organization.

What are the most important principles of nonviolence?

First, to be always attentive. Secondly, to be organized. Thirdly, to never lie. Fourthly, to not be afraid of death—to be willing to risk your life for revolutionary change.

How do you try to promote nonviolence?

One channel is through the diffusion of ideas, such as in books, classes, and seminars. But the more important way is through concrete action. I firmly believe that it is action that

---

This interview was conducted in São Paulo, by Mev Puleo, in June 1987, just months before the death of Fr. Barbé. It was translated by Mev Puleo.

forms persons — action that is later analyzed and evaluated. And for me, the greatest way to spread nonviolence is to link it to the grassroots struggle. To be effective in this struggle, we need teams that bring together lawyers, politicians, experts skilled in communications, and those with religious ties.

Most importantly, I never speak of nonviolence without proposing a concrete struggle. And, within this struggle, we must seek to "live" nonviolent combat, journeying with the mystique of loving our enemies.

What is the link between base ecclesial communities (CEBs) and nonviolent struggle?

The CEBs are a religious proposal to organize the people in their *barrios,* the first level of grassroots organization. Because of the faith-base, CEBs produce many persons who don't want to apply the death-inflicting rules of violent struggle. They want to live the struggle in an evangelical manner.

The Brazilian people, because of their deep Christianity, aren't very much in favor of using violence as an instrument of combat. The CEBs then evangelize with the Bible, reinforcing this tendency of nonviolence that's already present. Unfortunately, in spite of all this, nonviolence is not an institutional option of the Church yet.

Do you have much hope for nonviolence in Latin America today?

No one wants violence here. In Brazil, examples of armed conflicts, such as in Central America, terrify the people. Thus, no one's really preparing for armed struggle here, not even those groups that aren't directly linked with nonviolence. There may be small groups, but there aren't actually guerrilla groups here like "Sendero Luminoso" in Peru.

I also think there's a convergence of circumstances that could lead persons to embrace nonviolent combat as the most effective strategy. In this sense, there's a certain chance, especially when militants see it doesn't pay off to attack with arms that kill. We don't have enough arms to have a full armed conflict here. Thus, this particular sequence of events favors the progressive discovery of nonviolent alternatives.

Nevertheless, the groups that want change haven't actually

become convinced of this yet—neither the church nor the progressive groups. Thus far, we haven't managed to convince them that nonviolence is an effective alternative and that the right sequence of events justifies it.

Is the relationship between nonviolence and faith important?

In Brazil, yes. In practice, yes. That is, nonviolence isn't necessarily "religious," but it is part of a "creed," an act of faith in the intrinsic value of the human person. Even an atheist can have this vision of the absolute value of the human person. Practice reveals that almost always the practitioners of nonviolence have religious motivation. Faith is not a condition, however.

Is there something in your personal history that influenced you to pursue nonviolence?

It has been my religious faith. I'm not nonviolent merely for political efficacy. I believe that Christ's word to love one's enemies is completely empty if we don't apply it to social struggles. This belief brought me to nonviolence.

Do you believe that persons are sometimes forced to take up arms?

Yes, I believe it can be forced. That is, in some cases it is a lesser evil. Taking up arms, then, may not be a sin, but it is not evangelical. If I'm obliged to take up arms to defend a family, a child, a people (*povo*), I am going to say, "Unfortunately, I was obliged to take up arms." But, I never want to say it is evangelical—it is just an inevitable scandal. Like the phrase in the gospel, "It's inevitable that scandals will occur, but woe to those who cause them!" (Luke 17:1). That is, there are scandalous situations that cause persons to take up arms.

I also want to say that this violence occurs because there isn't a militancy active enough to organize an alternative. With foresight, there are always possibilities to mount a nonviolent way out. Without this foresight and organization, violence will prevail. Thus, violence comes from a lack of militancy in organizing a people.

Does the apathy of the majority also cause violence?

I believe that the greatest cause of collective violence is blind obedience to an unjust order. Those who tolerate the intolerable provoke such violence. This is true in the case of Argentina. The Argentine people is responsible for the massacres of those killed under the dictatorship because Argentinians remained passive, except the "crazies" of the Plaza de Mayo, the mothers of the disappeared, who resisted. The masses of Argentinians pursued a passivity that allowed torture and the massacres of many others to continue. It wasn't only the generals who were responsible.

In France, the masses of the French people, by their very passivity, were responsible for the persecution of the Jews. Just so, the Catholic Church by its passivity was responsible in part for the European war. Just so, the people of North America who don't do anything are actually responsible for the violence of a Reagan against the Third World. The foreign debt continues between the United States and Brazil and kills one thousand children a day. This comes from the politics of Reagan, but it also comes from the passivity of the people of the U.S.A.

Is the debt a form of violence?

Yes! It is institutional violence. The cheap sale of raw materials, our natural wealth, has paid for the debt. We have enriched the countries of the First World through financial groups operating in Brazil. This type of institutional violence kills millions of persons, many more than a world war.

Do you think the Third World should pay the debt?

Morally, we shouldn't pay. From the ethical point of view, we have already paid the debt many times over. We've paid too much! But politically, we have to look for other ways out, so as not to undermine the world market. But this would only be a political way out, demanded for the function of international business. It's not a moral demand.

What role do you see for the U.S.A. regarding nonviolence?

I don't expect anything from the U.S. government. From the people, Christians and non-Christians alike, I would like to see a much more militant attitude to fight against the two forms of disintegration: nuclear weapons and hunger. These are two faces of the same reality. They come from the same unjust system. Thus I hope that the people of the U.S.A. will be more militant in defense of life that is most threatened. Life that is most threatened is the moral barometer of history.

I also hope the people of the U.S.A. start a process of active struggle against the existing social system, working toward socialization of material and financial wealth. Both goods and money must be socialized and controlled in a way that does not injure the poor.

What message do you most want to share with the people of the United States?

I most want to say that the center of faith is our belief in the resurrection. This is the epitome of Christian faith: to believe in Christ who was raised from the dead. For us today the resurrection means that life is stronger than death, that good is greater than evil, that grace is stronger than dis-grace. Thus, I truly hope that the people of the U.S.A. don't take up a pessimistic vision of the world. Pessimism precedes conservatism. Pessimism doesn't try to change the established order, because it is afraid.

Those with the Christian optimism I speak of aren't afraid of change, because they believe in the power of life, which transforms. Thus my message would be that those who believe in the triumph of life, that they not be so afraid of death. Our great desire for resurrection will not prevail unless we overcome within ourselves the fear of death. It is better to die than to tolerate injustice. Those who are afraid of death remain pessimistic and conservative. We have to lose our fear of death and risk our lives for life to triumph.

Do you believe that wealth and consumerism deepen pessimism?

Everything that has to do with consumerism, by its very nature, obstructs love. You cannot serve two masters, luxury and the God of life. Impossible! Thus, those who cling to comfort, consumerized sexuality, food, and leisure, are not ready to risk their lives building new and better systems. These persons are very imprisoned. They're not willing to struggle.

You write about cultural idols in your books. What are the idols of our culture today?

I have no doubt that money is the principal idol of the West, of the capitalist world. In the East, it is power. I find that, in and of themselves, neither money nor power are able to create a new world. I believe that only the openness to divine grace allows a really radical change.

The idol of the West, money, unfolds into consumerism, leisure, and false tranquility. In order to defend these idols, Westerners have a trust—not just a blind trust, but a trust full of fear—in weapons. People know that weapons aren't very effective, but in spite of this they cling to these deadly weapons to defend the space in their lives given over to money.

In the Eastern countries, the people's idol is the state, as if the power of the state could be the principal source of happiness, as if it could "organize" happiness. But this isn't true. No state can organize happiness; true joy springs from something much deeper.

Does the Third World also have idols?

Yes. They have the tendency to adopt others' idols. There's a profound Marxist saying: "The dominant ideas are the ideas of the dominating class." Since the dominating class has everything at its fingertips, including its ideology and the means of communication, it passes its idols on to others, even to the poorest of peoples. However, reality reveals that these idols deceive; they don't bring about happiness.

All the *favelas* [shantytowns] have TVs. Looking at the TV, the poor can watch middle-class life, but they can't buy the life they see. Thus, the reality of their poverty demythifies the idols that the First World tries to pass on to them. At the same time, these idols manage to hold back the people's struggle. They disorganize and demobilize us by imposing false expectations.

In Brazil, we have "consumerism of misery." The people throw away money making payments on TVs—they put aside money or their TV will be cut off. The commercial system has a thousand ways to sell consumer goods to the poor through installments. Thus, the poor are bound to the seductive images of the media, but they're also bound by the money they owe.

They're also bound by the ideas that come through the TV.

The human being is a very fragile being—very emotional and very fragile. It's easy to destroy a human being. Thus, a system with all the ideological resources can manipulate and break even a very strong person.

You write about capitalism. Do you see it as a root of violence?

Yes. Any system that makes an absolute of that which isn't absolute is a root of violence. The function of idolatry is to put an object in the place of the image of God, which is the human person. For this reason, capitalism is institutionally perverse. Its perversity is hidden because at first glance one doesn't see this inversion. It is a perversity that seduces, that offers the privileges of life but actually destroys human relationships and our relationship with God as well—double destruction!

You recognize a crisis of faith in our world. Do you see more signs of atheism today?

I see very little of this in Brazil or the rest of Latin America. A little bit exists among the middle class, who suffer the shock of modernity even more than the poor. Atheism may come later on. But personally, I see that the crisis of faith comes in three successive moments. First, persons stop believing in God because they suffer so much. There is a lot of disgrace and injustice.

The second crisis of faith occurs when persons stop believing that it's worth the effort to dedicate themselves to a political cause. Ultimately, you need some ideal to believe in a political struggle, to believe that with human effort an activist can change society. Thus, a time could come when entire masses of citizens stop believing in the will to dedicate themselves to a political cause. This is the second faith that dies, faith in a cause.

After this, human love is still left. When religious faith and political faith are abandoned, the only faith left is faith in other persons, or love. Even this can be destroyed by consumerism and licentiousness, because when you buy and sell everything, including the human body, you cast a suspicion on love. Yes, the consumerism of sexuality casts a suspicion on love and from there doubt is born about this third faith, that of interpersonal and familial love.

When you have no love of God, no love in a political cause, and no love for a family, spouse or children, there is not much left. Suicide is left. This happens a lot in Europe and the more "advanced" countries. Drugs prevail. Drugs are a form of ecstasy, of getting outside oneself. It isn't enough to get out of misery, we also want to get outside of ourselves. Ecstasy is as necessary as food.

When there is nothing left of these three faiths, chemical ecstasy prevails — and suicide prevails, an escape from life through death. I believe we are in suicidal societies because we place ourselves in the center of the human search. We don't face the mystery of existence, which for me is the personal presence of God. Instead, we place the human being in the center, and inside the human being we put only pleasure. This leads to a complete disintegration of society.

The title of your book recently released in the U.S.A. is Grace and Power. *What is the relationship between grace and power?*

Power can merely organize sharing; it can't inspire sharing. Sharing springs from within the human person. It is an act of grace. No one can force this free self-gift of one to another. It's something that blossoms from within me or from within society.

For example, we have countless years of biblical tradition. It still flows from within the human person to stop on the highway when someone is wounded. This isn't just a spontaneous thing. It comes from an extensive biblical, Judeo-Christian education teaching us that the Samaritan is a fellow being. This is in the blood of many poor persons. In blindness we call this spontaneity, but it's the result of a long education of grace. This could disappear at any moment. Thus, without an enduring grace born from within the human person, no one can organize sharing. Power organizes things provided that there are people willing to share.

In the gospels we have the multiplication of bread. Here the atmosphere of sharing springs from the heart of Christ, which motivated the people to share their resources. In this sense, Jesus multiplied the resources because he found openness among the people. After that, he had people sit together in groups of fifty. Thus, the second moment of this gospel tells about power: the grouping and organization of persons. Power is important—however it is only a second moment, an instrument to organize once sharing has happened.

Is this similar to the difference between the mystical and the political?

It's almost the same. Politics is an important form of charity, of love. It reorganizes the rules of the social game in order to make a more human society. It helps define the rules of this game through a constitution. The tragedy in Brazil is that there is no constitution, not in people's heads nor in society. Thus, everyone lives in great confusion. For example, if cars circulate through a city without traffic rules, accidents happen. Politics seeks to organize the circulation of ideas, food, and other resources, so that no one is left out.

Mysticism is a mysterious thing. We Christians believe that human disgrace comes from a disturbed relationship with God. The relationship isn't destroyed, but is agitated by a serious crisis or an unhealthy relationship. This unhealthy relationship with God occurs between persons at the social level as well. This ailing social relationship is concretized in social structures that escape our control, structures that should be controlled by healthy politics.

But all of this comes from a damaged relationship with God. That's why we say we need a Savior—a revolution isn't enough to rectify the rules of the game. The liberation we preach includes the political, but it's also beyond it. Thus, we find human tragedy in political circumstances, but the real tragedy is greater. Just the same, human evil is deeper than political or economic evil.

The mystic is a person who is conscious of the *real* human tragedy—a religious tragedy—that is much more serious than a political or economic tragedy. The mystic feels this. The mystic doesn't disdain the political level, for he or she knows that to cure the religious we must reorganize the political level of existence as well. But it's also not enough to be a mystic to solve political questions. Spiritual illness is at the root of every illness, but political illness must still be cured with political means.

The great result of the struggle between the Vatican and liberation theology was to redefine the two dimensions of salvation. We have a radical and definitive salvation from sin and death that comes only through Christ who came to save us and cure this relationship. But we have another dimension of liberation that the liberation theologians call social liberation from the gravity of historical oppression. This is a specific dimension of integral liberation. It can't be separated from the first liberation, but it can't be confused with it either.

How are the base ecclesial communities (CEBs) affecting the church?

In Brazil, especially in São Paulo, all our pastoral work was oriented to promote the CEBs. To this day, all of our pastoral plans, all of the candidates selected for the priesthood, were made only if they accepted promotion of the CEBs. In Brazil, we can say that the official pastoral work of the church, of the CNBB [National Conference of Brazilian Bishops], is basically this: liberation theology, base communities, and all their consequences. All our ecclesial machinery is directed toward empowering the people. Now, this is only in general terms, for there is resistance in the church as well. However, the recent elections in the CNBB showed that this line will continue the trend of the past twenty years.

In your view, are the CEBs having an impact on the world church?

There is little evidence so far. Twenty years is still a short time for us to know this. There are historical examples that prove how powerful movements after twenty years of existence meet with such great resistance that they are destroyed. The greatest strength we have now is the hope of liberation theology, not what we read in books, but that which is incarnate, embodied in the people and the CEBs. It's much more difficult to restrict persons than it is to restrict books.

Roughly half of the Catholics in the world are in Latin America. Brazil is a country that leads the way in terms of CEBs. Thus, there is a certain hope that it won't be possible to govern the Catholic Church "against" the direction of Latin America and Brazil. If this happened, there would be a terrible collision. Thus, there's a reasonable chance that this life of the CEBs will continue. Brazil is half a continent and the church has to recognize this movement. In fact, the pope's last letter to the bishops of Brazil was along these lines. He said that liberation theology isn't only good but opportune, as long as it stays linked to the long tradition of the church.

You wrote in Grace and Power *that the church is neither a monarchy nor a democracy. How would you define the structure of the church?*

I would say it is a communion. For example, when we have a CEB meeting with twenty persons who want something and two persons who don't, I always say we can't simply pass over those two persons. Sometimes you need to converse or to fast and pray until you find consensus. In Christian theology, the minority has a part of the Holy Spirit. If we pass over a minority, we pass over a truth that the Holy Spirit wants to express through this minority. In this sense, we're not bourgeois. Bourgeois democracy is derived from the force of the majority over the minority. This is a bourgeois vision, not an ecclesial vision.

This rule of decision-making is a theological vision that holds unity as fundamental. In many groups, divisions are born when a majority imposes their law on a minority under the pretext of "democracy." In reality, it turns out to be the ones who are stronger, richer, and more educated who get to be the "majority." But persons who are weaker, less learned, and less capable of expressing themselves are often more prophetic. They are stifled from entering the debate and are thus easily overthrown. This creates a deep resentment within the minority. Therefore, I'm in favor of struggling until a certain unity or consensus is reached. This is the real definition of the church as communion.

In this communion, it is the least of the members, the less learned and thus more prophetic, who speak the truth. They don't just speak for themselves; the Holy Spirit speaks through them. Now, the difficult thing is that all of us are mixed. Thus, the person who speaks by the Holy Spirit may not have total clarity. No one speaks with pure clarity, because we are sinners. So we need a process of moral-spiritual purification and an intellectual effort to help us perceive the truth of the minority. This is what a church of communion is all about. It's neither democracy nor monarchy.

Now, the Roman Church tends to be a monarchy—bishops, priests, etc. The Protestant churches tend to a kind of democracy, copying modern bourgeois democracy. The Christian church should be neither one nor the other. This is my opinion.

Are you thinking of writing another book?

I never think about writing books, but responding to questions that may later become books. Actually, I'm trying to respond to a question right now: How is it that persons in various civilizations are captured by the Spirit of God? How was the divine Spirit received in the various traditions of humanity? It would be a book about spirituality.

Spirituality isn't just sitting around praying; it is knowing how to situate oneself to receive the Spirit of God. The divine is very sensitive; at the slightest impulse it could withdraw. On the other hand, the Spirit can come like a great force in a people or in currents of history. Thus, there are certain currents that attract the Spirit of God and there are other things that drive the Spirit away. So, I'm studying how the Spirit of God lets itself be seduced by certain types of behavior and how the Spirit flees from other types of behavior in various traditions, religions, and geographical areas.

I may call this work *God of Life*. That is, how the life of God is flowing in humanity and what are the conditions for God's coming and remaining with us. It would be like a small sample of "mystical liberation theology." But I don't know how it will turn out. I work on it now and then; but I need to fast and pray, ask for God's help and converse with others about it. A book is very mysterious. No one knows how it will turn out.

In closing, what are your greatest hopes personally?

I have always, always wanted to see God. My greatest desire is to see God. I'm not resigned to *not* seeing God—it's unbearable. But I also know why we don't see God. It's written in the Bible that "only pure hearts will see God" and "blest are the pure of heart for they will see God." That which purifies a person isn't fasting, it's love. The only purifying force is love—not sentimental love, but love that truly wants good for others.

"Donating" is an attitude of the rich. There's a great saint who says something like, "Who are you that you have the audacity to donate?" It isn't enough to distribute what you have, but if you have a piece of clothing you should divide it in two. The lack of sharing shows that you have more than what you need. If you see someone in need, don't donate to them but share of yourself. Gandhi said that the person who has something and doesn't use it is like a thief. The person who has only what he or she needs can't give, because of their own need, but they should divide what they have.

Love doesn't "donate"; it divides, distributes, shares. Love shares at all levels: personal, theological, cultural. This sharing doesn't come from a capacity to organize; it comes from the creativity of love. Equality is fundamental to love. Love is not paternalistic.

The only thing that keeps us from seeing God is that we love very little. And we don't love because it's extremely difficult to part with our possessions. We resist giving up the smallest things—a shirt we like or giving time to the persons who drop in on us. It is difficult to give up things and persons. This binds us.

The fact that Jesus had no place to recline his head is not to say he was poor, but that he was totally available to others. He wasn't tied down by anything. This is more difficult for the rich. The rich are captives, slaves to many things that bind them like glue, things that keep them from giving. They aren't open to being dislocated. Thus, they are victims. All the good things they have turn into chains—too much food, cars, money. They try to satisfy themselves with these things and lose their spiritual gift in the process.

Our great Judeo-Christian tradition tells us that the greatest force of revolution is love—not sentimental love, but mystical love. This is the greatest thing in the Judeo-Christian biblical tradition. Our great prophets and saints, like Martin Luther King and Gandhi, Oscar Romero and Francis of Assisi, these are the ones who lived this tradition more faithfully. Thus, they give us hope. Others recognize themselves in this mirror. They recognize that their deepest nature shines forth from these saints and prophets.

All of this is very difficult because talking isn't enough; we have to actually help others. The great mystic St. John of the Cross said it is of little importance what ties us down, a rope or a thread. A tiny thread can keep a bird from flying. Thus, we have to cut away the things that hold us back.

The poor are different. Their very situation has cut away at what would keep them from sharing. Poverty certainly has its negative aspects — it can make persons hopeless. But it can also "spiritualize" persons, such as those tough, demanding persons who return to the essential, love.

I don't desire economic poverty for anyone. I desire evangelical poverty, which is a consciousness of not being tied down by anything, to be better able to love others. Capitalist poverty is diabolical. Evangelical poverty is mystical, a certain consciousness constructed day by day. This evangelical poverty doesn't come from capitalist poverty; it comes from a human tradition that calls on God in one's human poverty. Thanks be to God, even within diabolical poverty, one can survive by grace, holding onto love of others and love of God.

Notes

CHAPTER 1

1. René Girard, *Des choses cachées depuis la fondation du monde* (Paris: Grasset, 1979).
2. Ibid., p. 35.
3. Ibid., p. 40.
4. Ibid., p. 35.
5. Ibid., p. 55.
6. Michel Mabbesoli, "Les arcanes de la violence," *Supplement à la Vie Spirituelle,* November 1980, pp. 474, 476.
7. Torturers, those specialists in social sacrifice, typically cannot bring themselves to torture anyone without first being subjected to a brainwashing themselves, a "conscience-formation." "Your victims are monsters. Their crimes are unspeakable. Torture them and you will gain information that will save hundreds of lives," and so on.
8. This innocence can be total or relative. But any self-respecting society must esteem and defend whatever innocence there may be in the accused. This is the great and noble task of the judiciary. Without it, the society in question will become an assembly of executioners, and will function according to the principles of human sacrifice and the scapegoat.

CHAPTER 2

1. René Girard, *Des choses cachées,* p. 25.
2. Ibid., p. 31.
3. R. Firth, *Tikopia Ritual and Belief,* as cited in Girard, *Des choses cachées,* p. 116.

CHAPTER 3

1. Joseph has inherited the shrewdness of his father Jacob. He always thinks things out in advance, as we see in his later conduct with

179

regard to his brother Benjamin. The famous novelist, Thomas Mann, in *Joseph and His Brethren,* presents Potiphar's wife as sincerely passionate, and Joseph as cold and calculating.

2. We find the same antisacrificial spirit in the Bible's rejection of the sacrifice of Isaac.

3. René Girard, *Des choses cachées,* p. 178.

CHAPTER 4

1. René Girard, *Des choses cachées,* p. 203.
2. The source of the title of Girard's book.
3. A. Dumas, writing in *La Vie Spirituelle,* vol. 85 (May 1968).
4. Girard, *Des choses cachées,* p. 234.
5. Ibid., p. 241.

CHAPTER 5

1. The essentials of the ideas set forth in this chapter are taken from Jacques Sémelin, *Pour sortir de la violence* (Paris: Duvrières).
2. Sémelin, *Pour sortir de la violence.*
3. Hannah Arendt, *Eichmann in Jerusalem,* as cited in Sémelin, *Pour Sortir de la violence,* p. 58. Arendt herself is Jewish, and above any suspicion of partiality in her selection or assessment of the facts.
4. Bruno Bettelheim, as cited in Sémelin, p. 60.
5. Hannah Arendt, as cited in Sémelin, p. 77.
6. H. G. Adler, *Theresienstadt 1941–1945* (Tübingen, 1955).
7. As cited in Sémelin, p. 77.
8. Ibid., p. 81.
9. Ibid., p. 78.

CHAPTER 8

1. Fernando Belo, *Leitura política do evangelho.*
2. Ibid., p. 94.
3. Ibid.

CHAPTER 10

1. Alfred Kuntz, a priest of the Sons of Charity, who had been in Crateús for fifteen years, himself a nonviolent activist.
2. Note the original exegesis of this popular piety. It has turned

"If you are the Son of God" (Matt. 27:40) from derision to faith, and "His blood be on us" (Matt. 27:25) from curse to blessing.

CHAPTER 11

1. As cited in José Comblin, *Théologie de la révolution* (Paris, 1968).
2. C. Grinberg, *Histoire universelle,* 10:16.
3. Babylon represents the "city of man" in its evil aspect. Jerusalem is the archetype of the contrary, which must become reality. Urban life as such is not condemned.
4. J. M. Muller, *L'Evangile de la non-violence.*
5. Leonardo Boff, *Jesus Christ Liberator: A Critical Christology for Our Time* (Maryknoll, N.Y.: Orbis, 1978), pp. 49–62: "What Did Jesus Christ Really Want?"
6. Many non-Christians, as well, practice an "open religion." Gandhi would be an example.
7. Mohandas K. Gandhi, *Minha Experiência com a Verdade* (Rio de Janeiro: Editorial Cruziero).